GW00890277

The **Big Book**
of
National Insults

The **Big**

Book
of
National Insults

Julian L'Estrange

CASSELL

This edition first published in the UK 2002 by
Cassell
Wellington House
125 Strand
London WC2R oBB

British Library Cataloguing in Publication Data
A catalogue record for this book is available
from the British Library

ISBN 0-304-35789-8

Distributed in the United States by
Sterling Publishing Co. Inc.
387 Park Avenue South
New York, NY 10016, USA

Design by Harry Green
Printed by MPG Books Ltd, Bodmin, Cornwall

Contents

Introduction

Love it or loathe it, Abroad is here (or, actually, *there*) to stay. What constitutes Abroad, and therefore defines what is Foreign, may vary from the far Antipodes to the end of the street – as was observed in *Punch* the century before last (was it really so long ago?):

> Who's 'im, Bill?
> A stranger!
> 'Eave 'arf a brick at 'im.

They say that the world is shrinking, that we're all globalized now, that all men (and women) are brothers (or, technically, siblings). But do we detect a diminution in prejudice and bile in this Enlightened Age? We do not. The backwoodsmen (backwoods*persons*) of the Tory Party and their like are as barking as ever they were, snarling rabidly across the Channel. 'No! No! No!' they shriek with Mrs Thatcher, like elderly virgins declining a ravishing. As Tony Parsons once wrote:

> To be born an Englishman – ah, what an easy conceit that
> builds in you, what a self-righteous nationalism, a secure
> xenophobia, what a pride in your ignorance.

But the English are by no means as unique in this respect as we might think. In the USA the *National Lampoon* keeps its finger on the country's pulse:

> With its open-door immigration policy, the United States is

perhaps the only state not afflicted with xenophobia, but
the very warp and weave of our national fiber [No, they
can't spell, can they? Ed.] is even now being eaten away by
swarms of wops, dps, prs, coons and foreigners generally.
At the same time the *Lampoon* dispassionately surveys national attitudes around the world:

Chauvinism is a French word which cannot be translated, so
Froggie is the emotion it describes.

If this little volume goes to show anything, it is that, wherever
you live, whatever your nationality, *them over there* are not like
us over here. When you have read the Yanks on the Brits, the
Brits on the Yanks, the Germans on the Poles, the Poles on the
Germans, the Irish on the English, the English on the Irish, the
Illyrians on the Italians, the Ukrainians on the Russians, the
Portuguese on the Spanish, the French on the French, and vir-
tually every other possible combination of mutual enmity,
you'll realize this single truth: *We're all as bad as each other!*

As Arthur 'Ol' Misery Guts' Schopenhauer once grumbled,
'Every nation ridicules other nations, and all are right.'

Oh *Schadenfreude*!!

JULIAN L'ESTRANGE
Dungivinadam
Waterloo Road, Stoke Newington

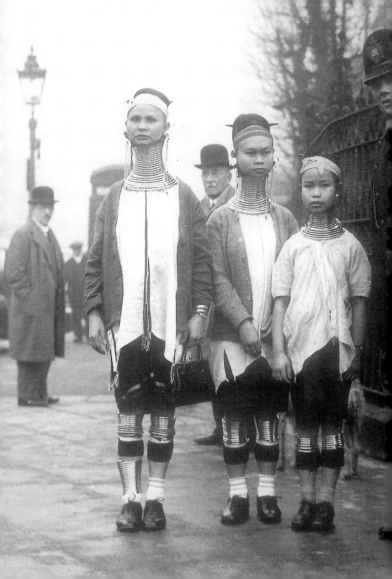

Prologue

Foreigners are Fiends

Abroad is unutterably bloody and foreigners are fiends.

Uncle Matthew, in Nancy Mitford's *The Pursuit of Love* (1945)

In the same book, Uncle Matthew declares:

I loathe abroad, nothing would induce me to live there ... and, as for foreigners, they are all the same, and they all make me sick.

Uncle Matthew was slightly more extreme than King George VI, who pronounced merely that –

Abroad is bloody.

King George VI, attributed in W.H. Auden, *A Certain World: A Commonplace Book* (1970)

Confound their politics,
Frustrate their knavish tricks.

'God Save the King' (mid-18th century), attributed to Henry Carey and others

For anything I see, foreigners are fools.

Hugo Meynell (1727–80), quoted in James Boswell, *Life of Samuel Johnson* (1791)

Who's 'im, Bill?
A stranger!
'Eave 'arf a brick at 'im.

Anonymous cartoon in *Punch*, 25 February 1854

Not Cricket

And all the world over, each nation's the same,
They've simply no notion of playing the game;
They argue with umpires, they cheer when
 they've won,
And they practise beforehand, which ruins the fun.
Michael Flanders, with Donald Swann, 'A Song of
Patriotic Prejudice', from *At the Drop of Another Hat*
(1963)

If Stalin had learned to play cricket, the world
might now be a better place.
Richard Downey (1881–1953), English bishop, in 1948

I often think how much easier the world would
have been to manage if Herr Hitler and Signor
Mussolini had been to Oxford.
Viscount Halifax, speech, in York, 4 November 1937

If any of you have got an A-level, it is because you have
worked to get it. Go to any other country and when you
have got an A-level, you have bought it.
Michael Portillo, when chief secretary to the Treasury, in an
address to students at Southampton University, 4 February 1994

The great and recurrent question about abroad is, is it worth getting there?

Rose Macaulay (1881–1958), British novelist

The British tourist is always happy abroad as long as the natives are waiters.

Robert Morley, quoted in the *Observer*, 20 April 1958

With its open-door immigration policy, the United States is perhaps the only state not afflicted with xenophobia, but the very warp and weave of our national fiber is even now being eaten away by swarms of wops, dps, prs, coons and foreigners generally.

The National Lampoon Encyclopedia of Humor (1968)

Comparisons are Odious

... but irresistible.

**And crossing the Channel, one cannot say much
For the French or the Spanish, the Danish or Dutch –
The Germans are German, the Russians are Red,
And the Greeks and Italians eat garlic in bed.**

Michael Flanders, with Donald Swann, 'A Song of Patriotic Prejudice', from *At the Drop of Another Hat* (1963)

In the eyes of the Englishman, the Frenchman is a dog, the Spaniard a fool, the German a drunkard, the Italian a bandit; only the Englishman is the pinnacle of perfection, and nature's masterpiece.

A. Riem (1762–1828)

Among three Italians will be found two clergymen; among three Spaniards, two braggarts; among three Germans, two soldiers; among three Frenchmen, two chefs; and among three Englishmen, two whoremongers.

German saying

The points i wish to make about the world are contained in the molesworth newsletter.
(a) the russians are roters.
(b) americans are swankpots.
(c) the french are slack.
(d) the germans are unspeakable.
(e) the rest are as bad if not worse than the above.
(f) the british are brave super and noble cheers cheers cheers.

Geoffrey Whillans and Ronald Searle, 'Down With Skool!', *The Compleet Molesworth* (1958)

I thought for a moment I had discovered a straightforward inverse correlation between nations and their food-and-drink. Spanish, like English, nice people, nasty food; French, nasty people, nice food. Oh yes, and Greeks, nice people, terrifying food. But then, Italians, nice people, nice food. Danes too. Surely there must be ... Got it: Germans, nasty people, nasty food (drink better, but beer overrated, wine no good with food, schnappses often delicious but not enough on

their own). Also Belgians – Walloons anyway. So
no little article there.

Kingsley Amis, 'Amis Abroad', in the *Spectator*, 23
November 1963

There have been many definitions of hell, but for
the English the best definition is that it is a
place where the Germans are the police, the
Swedish are the comedians, and the Italians are
the defence force, Frenchmen dig the roads, the
Belgians are the pop singers, the Spanish run
the railways, the Turks cook the food, the Irish
are the waiters, the Greeks run the government
and the common language is Dutch.

David Frost and Antony Jay, *To England with Love*
(1967)

Speaking English When Our Backs are Turned

I don't hold with abroad and think that
foreigners speak English when our backs are
turned.

Quentin Crisp, *The Naked Civil Servant* (1968)

Abroad is full of people who have the discourtesy of
persisting in speaking their own language:
Foreigners may pretend otherwise, but if English
is spoken loudly enough, anyone can understand
it, the British included. Actually, there's no such
thing as a foreign language. The world is just

filled with people who grunt and squeak instead of speaking sensibly. French may be an exception. But since it's impossible to figure out what French people are saying, we'll never know for sure.

P.J. O'Rourke, *Modern Manners* (1983)

There is the fear, common to all English-only speakers, that the chief purpose of foreign languages is to make fun of us.

Barbara Ehrenreich, *The Worst Years of Our Lives*, 'Language Barrier' (1991)

Everybody has the right to pronounce foreign names as he chooses.

Winston Churchill, quoted in the *Observer*, 5 August 1951

I went first to Germany, and there I spoke with the German Foreign Minister, Herr … Herr and there. And we exchanged many frank words in our respective languages.

Peter Cook, giving his impersonation of Harold Macmillan, in *Beyond the Fringe* (1961)

The Devilish Thing about Foreign Affairs

This is the devilish thing about foreign affairs: they are foreign and will not always conform to our whim.

James Reston, in the *New York Times*, 16 December 1964

Diplomacy. The art of saying 'Nice Doggie!' till you can find a rock.

Wynn Catlin (1930–), American writer

I asked Tom if countries always apologized when
they had done wrong, and he says: 'Yes; the little
ones does.'
Mark Twain, *Tom Sawyer Abroad* (1894)

Alliance, n. In international politics, the union of two
thieves who have their hands so deeply in each other's
pocket that they cannot separately plunder a third.
Ambrose Bierce, *The Devil's Dictionary* (1906)

Peace, n. In international affairs, a period of cheating
between two periods of fighting.
Ambrose Bierce, *The Devil's Dictionary* (1906)

Conferences at the top level are always courteous.
Name-calling is left to the foreign ministers.
W. Averell Harriman (1891–1986), American diplomat,
remark in 1955

The great nations have always acted like gangsters
and the small nations like prostitutes.
Stanley Kubrick, in the *Guardian*, 5 June 1963

If you start throwing hedgehogs under me, I shall
throw two porcupines under you.
Nikita Khrushchev, apparently repeating a Russian proverb,
quoted in the *New York Times*, 7 November 1963

The only thing the member states of the UN have in
common is their ability to see one another's faults.
Laurence J. Peter, *Quotations for Our Time* (1977)

On National Repugnancies

**We cannot bring ourselves to believe it possible
that a foreigner should in any respect be wiser than
ourselves. If any such point out to us our follies,
we at once claim those follies as the special evidences
of our wisdom.**

Anthony Trollope, *Orley Farm* (1862)

**Every nation thinks its own madness normal and
requisite; more passion and more fancy it calls folly,
less it calls imbecility.**

George Santayana, *Dialogues in Limbo* (1925)

Every nation ridicules other nations, and all are right.

Arthur Schopenhauer (1788–1860), notably pessimistic
German philosopher

Europe

A Continent of Mongrels

Purity of race does not exist. Europe is a continent of energetic mongrels.
H.A.L. Fisher, *A History of Europe* (1935)

A worn-out portion of the globe.
Lord Byron, letter, 3 October 1819

Races north of the Pyrenees never reach maturity; they are of a great stature and of a white colour. But they lack all sharpness of wit and penetration and intellect.
Saïd of Toledo, Moorish traveller, in *c.* 1100

Crimes, Follies and Misfortunes

On whatever side we regard the history of Europe, we shall perceive it to be a tissue of crimes, follies, and misfortunes.
Oliver Goldsmith, *The Citizen of the World* (1762)

What else is Europe but a conglomeration of mistakes? Mistakes that are so diverse that they complement each other and balance one another. Taken separately, we're each unbearable in our own way.
Hans Enzensberger, 'Polish Incidents' (1987)

The only cultural heritage that the 321 peoples of Europe share is that of America. That is why the organizers of Euro-Disneyland are on safe ground.
Kenneth Hudson, English museums expert, in 1990

Europhobia

Two or three winters ago a heavy storm completely blocked traffic across the Channel. 'CONTINENT ISOLATED', the newspapers couldn't help saying.
John Gunther, *Inside Europe* (1938)

Baldwin thought Europe was a bore, and Chamberlain thought it was only a greater Birmingham.
Winston Churchill, in 1953. Neville Chamberlain, who succeeded Baldwin as prime minister in 1937, had been lord mayor of Birmingham earlier in his career.

Of the first proposals for a European Parliament:
When you open that Pandora's box you will find if full of Trojan 'orses.
Ernest Bevin, British foreign secretary (1945–51)

This 'going in to Europe' will not turn out to be the thrilling mutual exchange supposed. It is more like middle-aged couples with failing marriages meeting in a darkened bedroom in a Brussels hotel for a group grope.
E.P. Thomson, during the referendum on British membership of the European Community, 1975

What Caesar couldn't do, what Charlemagne couldn't do, what Innocent III and Hitler couldn't do, it looks like the dough-faced burgher wimps of Brussels might finally be able to pull off – the unification of that portion of the Earth's surface known ... as Europe. What it took a country ten times its size less than a hundred years to accomplish, armed with only machine guns and a few trillion dollars, it has taken the squabbling, babbling tribes of Europe almost three millennia of wars, migrations, crusades, plague, pillage, partition, diets, dumas, duels, vendettas, incursions, invasions, intrusions, regicides, switching sides and genocide to accomplish.

Tony Hendra, 'EEC! It's the US of E!', in *National Lampoon*, 1976

The last time Britain went into Europe with any degree of success was on 6 June 1944.

Daily Express, 1980

Europe is a place teeming with ill-intentioned persons.

Margaret Thatcher

Gloria, gloria, Europhoria!
Common faith and common goal!
Meat and milk and wine and butter
Make a smashing casserole!
Let the end of all our striving
Be the peace that love promotes,
With our hands in perfect friendship
Firmly round each other's throats!

Roger Woddis, in the *Spectator*, 1984

Of the European Parliament:
This place needs a laxative.
Bob Geldof, in 1985

UP YOURS, DELORS
Sun headline, November 1990, referring to Jacques Delors, the
French president of the Commission of the European
Community in the 1980s, who initiated the Delors Plan for
greater European union.

Filthy Foreign Food: I

**Another article of cuisine that offends the
bowels of unused Britons is garlic. Not
uncommonly in southern climes an egg with
a shell on is the only procurable animal food
without garlic in it. Flatulence and looseness
are the frequent results.**
Dr T.K. Chambers, *A Manual of Diet in Health and
Disease* (1875)

**Britain does not wish to be ruled by a conglomerate in
Europe which includes Third World nations such as the
Greeks and Irish, nor for that matter the Italians and
French, whose standards of political morality are not
ours, and never will be.**
Alfred Sherman, in 1990

It's a German racket to take over the whole of Europe. You might as well give it to Hitler.
Nicholas Ridley, referring to the European Community in the *Spectator*, 14 July 1990. The remark led to his resignation from Mrs Thatcher's government.

SOD THE EU – HOME RULE FOR BRITAIN
Bumper sticker sported by a Shropshire squire, observed by Jeremy Paxman in *The English* (1998)

No! No! No!
Margaret Thatcher, opposing a single European currency and greater central control from Brussels, House of Commons, 30 October 1990

The French are a nation of collaborators ... Germany's unique contribution to Europe has been to plunge it into two World Wars ... French wine is mostly inferior to that of Australia but in their own rule-twisting way it's probably hard for the French to find that out for themselves ... The purpose of the Government's European policy is to avoid being thrown into some bastardized, federalized, European destiny, actively and fawningly crawling to France and Germany as the lesser countries insult us to the tune of their begging bowls ... I wish I was not in the Community.
Patrick Nicholls, in the *Western Morning News*, 23 November 1994. He resigned as vice-chairman of the Conservative Party the same day.

A Great Big Garbage Pail:
Views from America

'When I was your age,' my mother said, 'I ate herring and black bread for thirty-six days in the bottom of a ship to get from Antwerp to New York. Outside of New York there's nothing. Only a great big garbage pail they call Europe.'

Jerome Weidman, *Praying for Rain* (1986)

Filthy Foreign Food: II

On the Continent the household bread is usually unwholesome and nasty, and captain's biscuits are never to be obtained. It is prudent to carry a store of them to use when the staff of life is found especially abominable.

Dr T.K. Chambers, *A Manual of Diet in Health and Disease* (1875)

Can we never extract the tapeworm of Europe from the brain of our countrymen?

Ralph Waldo Emerson, *The Conduct of Life*, 'Culture' (1860)

That Europe's nothin' on earth but a great big auction, that's all it is.

Tennessee Williams, *Cat on a Hot Tin Roof* (1955)

Whatever it is I read about Europe is war. Them white men is always fightin'. War'a the Roses, the Crewsades, the Revolution, the Kaiser, Hitler, the com'unists. Shit! All they care 'bout, war an' money, money an' land.

Walter Mosley, *A Red Death* (1991)

Filthy Foreign Food: III

Continental breakfasts are very sparse, usually just a pot of coffee or tea and a teensy roll that looks like a suitcase handle. My advice is to go right to lunch without pausing.

Miss Piggy, *Miss Piggy's Guide to Life (As Told to Henry Beard)* (1981)

France: A Nation Protected by a Cloud of Garlic

Probably the worst xenophobes on earth are the French, a nation protected by a cloud of garlic breath which still built the Maginot Line to keep foreigners out. Chauvinism is a French word which cannot be translated, so Froggie is the emotion it describes.
The National Lampoon Encyclopedia of Humor (1973)

They are a short blue-vested people who carry their own onions when cycling abroad, and have a yard which is 3.37 inches longer than other people's.
Alan Coren, *The Sanity Inspector* (1974)

Basically the French are all peasants.
Pablo Picasso, remark, 16 February 1935

Have the Frenchman for thy friend, not for thy neighbour.
Nicephorus I, Byzantine emperor

Frogs, Frenchies and Oui-Ouis

Frogs, the commonest derogatory term for the French, was first applied (in the 17th century) to the Dutch, England's number-one enemy at the time. When in the 18th century the Dutch were replaced by the French as least-liked foreigners, it was the French who became the Frogs. *Froggies* and *Frogeaters* were later refinements, and *Jiggle-and-Jogs* is a rhyming-slang version. Inevitably, France is *Frogland*, or, in New Zealand, *Frogolia* (where the French themselves are *Frogolians*).

An amphibious 19th-century variant of *Frog* is *Crappo*, from the French *crapaud*, a toad. A *Frenchie*, as well as being a French person, is also, in US slang, a foolish man or a flighty woman. Other slang terms for the French include *Oui-Oui* (or *Wee-Wee*), and *Parleyvoo*.

French Letters

There is a treasure-trove of slang insultingly associated with France and the French.

In the 1920s, in the Caribbean, *France* became a euphemism for 'fuck' or 'hell', as in such phrases as 'What the France are you on about?' Apparently the usage originated in the terrible experiences of West Indian soldiers serving in France in World War I.

By far the largest number of slang terms involving the word 'French' are to do with sex, echoing the old belief that the immodest French are at it often and in every conceivable way.

Oral sex (*French tricks*) would appear to be particularly popular. *To French* is to fellate, and *French art*, *French culture*, *French head job*, *French love* and *French way* are all terms for fellatio. *French fuck* and *French wank* are both terms for rubbing the penis between a woman's breasts. A *French kiss* (one with lots of tongue action) seems quite chaste in comparison.

While indulging in these kinds of activities, it might be as well to wear a *French cap* or *French letter*, more familiarly known as just a *frenchie*, or, in Australia, a *frog* or *frogskin*. For extra stimulation, you might try on a *French tickler*. The use of such condoms will contain a man's *French dressing* (aka *French-fried ice-cream*). They might also prevent infection with the *French disease*, otherwise named the *Frenchman*, *French crown*, *French goods*, *French gout*, *French marbles*, *French measles* or *French pig* or *pox*. As the German saying goes, 'French pox and a leather vest wear for life.'

Idle Monkeys: The French on the French

Your nation is divided into two species: one is of idle monkeys mocking at everything; the other is of tigers who tear.

Voltaire, himself a Frenchman, writing of the French in a letter to Mme du Deffand, 21 November 1766

A nation of monkeys with the throats of parrots.

Joseph Sieyès (1748–1836), letter to Mirabeau

A little of everything and nothing thoroughly, after the French fashion.

Michel de Montaigne (1533–92), *Essays*, I, 26

The French complain of everything and always.

Napoleon I. In a speech in 1813 Napoleon declared 'France has more need of me than I have need of France' – a risky assertion at a time when his military fortunes were fast failing.

We all have the republican spirit in our veins, like syphilis in our bones. We are democratized and venerealized.

Charles Baudelaire (1821–67), epilogue to *Sur la Belgique*

I am bored with France, particularly as everybody here resembles Voltaire.

Charles Baudelaire, 'Mon Coeur mis à nu', *Journaux intimes* (1887)

The ignorance of French society gives one a rough sense of the infinite.

Ernest Renan (1823–92), philosopher and historian

The English are crooked as a nation and honest as individuals. The contrary is true of the French, who are honest as a nation and crooked as individuals.

Edmond and Jules de Goncourt, *The Goncourt Journals* (1888–96)

I have tried to lift France out of the mud. But she will return to her errors and vomitings. I cannot prevent the French from being French.

Charles de Gaulle, quoted in *Time*, 8 December 1967

The Entente Not-So-Very-Cordiale

France is a dog-hole.

William Shakespeare, *All's Well That Ends Well*, II.iii

'Tis better using France than trusting France.

William Shakespeare, *Henry VI, Part 3*, IV.i

Why, is it not a lamentable thing, grandsire, that we should be thus afflicted with these strange flies, these fashion-mongers, these perdona-mi's?

William Shakespeare, *Romeo and Juliet*, II.iv

**The faithless vain disturber of mankind,
Insulting Gaul.**

James Thomson, *The Seasons*, 'Autumn' (1726–30)

**I hate the French because they are all slaves, and wear
wooden shoes.**

Oliver Goldsmith, *Essays*, 24, 'Distresses of a Common Soldier'

You must hate a Frenchman as you hate the devil.

Horatio, Lord Nelson, quoted in Robert Southey,
Life of Nelson (1813)

**I say to you that you are better than a Frenchman. I
would lay even money that you who are reading this
are more than five feet seven in height, and weigh
eleven stone; while a Frenchman is five feet four and
does not weigh nine. The Frenchman has after his soup
a dish of vegetables, where you have one of meat. You
are a different and superior animal – a French-beating
animal (the history of hundreds of years has shown
you to be so).**

William Makepeace Thackeray, quoted in George Orwell,
Charles Dickens (1939)

**The best thing I know between France and England is –
the sea.**

Douglas Jerrold, *The Wit and Opinions of Douglas Jerrold*, 'The
Anglo-French Alliance' (1859)

THE COMTE D'ORSAY: **I was born French, have lived French and
will die French.**
BENJAMIN DISRAELI: **Have you no ambition, man?**

Paris is Like a Whore

Paris is like a whore. From a distance she seems ravishing, you can't wait until you have her in your arms. Five minutes later you feel empty, disgusted with yourself. You feel tricked.
Henry Miller

To err is human. To loaf is Parisian.
Victor Hugo, *Les Misérables* (1862)

Paris is the paradise of the easily impressed – the universal provincial mind.
Robert Elms, quoted in Julie Burchill, *Sex and Sensibility* (1992)

Cities are only human. And I had begun to see Paris for the bitch she is: a stunning transvestite – vain, narrow-minded and all false charm.
Irma Kurtz, in the *Daily Mail*, 1996

The most frivolous and fickle of civilized nations.
Walter Bagehot, *Literary Studies*, 'Shakespeare' (1879–95)

**Oh, how I love Humanity,
With love so pure and pringlish,
And how I hate the horrid French,
Who never will be English!**
G.K. Chesterton, 'The World State', from *Collected Poems* (1933)

The Almighty in His infinite wisdom did not see fit to create Frenchmen in the image of Englishmen.

Winston Churchill, speech, House of Commons, 10 December 1942

Frogs ... are slightly better than Huns or Wops.

Uncle Matthew, in Nancy Mitford's *The Pursuit of Love* (1945)

So damn your food and damn your wines,
Your twisted loaves and twisting vines,
Your *table d'hôte,* your *à la carte* ...
From now on you can keep the lot.
Take every single thing you've got,
Your land, your wealth, your men, your dames,
Your dream of independent power,
And dear old Konrad Adenauer,
And stick them up your Eiffel Tower.

Antony Jay, verse on de Gaulle's veto of Britain's application to join the Common Market, in *Time*, 8 February 1963

France has for centuries blocked our way to Europe. Before the invention of the aeroplane we had to step over it to get anywhere.

Robert Morley

The French are a logical people, which is one reason the English dislike them so intensely. The other is that they own France, a country which we have always judged to be much too good for them.

Robert Morley, *A Musing Morley*, 'France and the French' (1974)

The overall impression from the British and the Germans is that they love France itself but would rather that the French didn't live there.
Anonymous spokesman for the Paris Chamber of Commerce, referring to the results of a tourist survey

Britain has football hooligans, Germany has neo-Nazis, and France has farmers.
The Times, 1992

The French hate anything that is ugly. If they see an animal that is ugly, they immediately eat it.
Jeremy Clarkson

If the French won't buy our lamb, we won't use their letters.
Graffito on the back of a lorry during an Anglo-French 'lamb war' of 1980.

They Don't Understand Their Own Language

It is always a mistake trying to speak French to the Frogs. As Noël Coward once remarked when he was sustaining a role at the Comédie-Française, 'They don't understand their own language.'
Robert Morley

It is the true and native language of insincerity.
Alfred Sutro (1863–1933), *A Marriage Has Been Arranged*

'*Faute* de what?'
'*Mieux*, m'lord. A French expression. We should say
"For want of anything better."'
'What asses these Frenchmen are. Why can't they talk
English?'
'They are possibly more to be pitied than censured,
m'lord. Early upbringing no doubt has a lot to do
with it.'

P.G. Wodehouse, *Ring for Jeeves* (1953)

'Du ye think the Almighty would be understanin' siccan
gibberish?' said the old Scotch lady, when, during the
Napoleonic war, she was reminded that maybe a
French mother was praying as fervently for victory as
she was herself.

F.A. Steel

If the French were really intelligent they would speak
English.

Wilfred Sheed, 'Taking Pride in Prejudice', in *GQ*, 1984

[The French] gibber like baboons even when you try to
speak to them in their own wimpy language.

P.J. O'Rourke, 'Foreigners Around the World', in *National
Lampoon*, 1976

No matter how politely and distinctly you ask a
Parisian a question, he will persist in answering you
in French.

Fran Lebowitz, *Metropolitan Life* (1978)

One Englishman Can Beat Three Frenchmen

The saying 'One Englishman can beat three Frenchmen' has been dated to the late 16th century.

A fighting Frenchman runs away from even a she-goat.
Russian saying

When, at a formal reception, some senior French officers turned their backs on him:
I have seen their backs before.
The Duke of Wellington. In the Napoleonic Wars, the English slang term for a Frenchman was Jimmy Rend – from the French *je me rends*, 'I surrender'.

When the French fight for mankind they are wonderful. Whey they fight for themselves, they are nothing.
André Malraux, quoted in Bruce Chatwin, *What am I Doing Here?*, 'André Malraux' (1989)

I have not always in my dealings with General de Gaulle found quotations from Trafalgar and Waterloo necessarily productive, and he has been very tactful about the Battle of Hastings.
Harold Wilson, remark, 1967

Something Vichy about the French

There's something Vichy about the French.
Ivor Novello, quoted in a letter by Edward Marsh, March 1941.
Novello was parodying Noël Coward's 'There's Always
Something Fishy about the French' (quoted below).

When the Frenchman sleeps, the devil rocks him.
French saying

**The Frenchman's legs are thin, his soul little; he's
fickle as the wind.**
Russian saying

**France has neither winter nor summer nor morals –
apart from these drawbacks it is a fine country.**
Mark Twain, *Notebook* (pub. 1935)

**The Frenchman ... is likeable often just because of his
weaknesses, which are always thoroughly human,
even if despicable.**
Henry Miller, *The Wisdom of the Heart*, 'Raimu' (1941)

Sex Pervades the Air

**One becomes aware in France, after having lived in
America, that sex pervades the air. It's there all around
you, like a fluid.**
Henry Miller, interview in *Writers at Work* (Second Series, 1963,
ed. George Plimpton)

The confident and over-lusty French.
William Shakespeare, *Henry V*, IV, prologue

It is unthinkable for a Frenchman to arrive at middle age without having syphilis and the Croix de la Légion d'Honneur.

André Gide. Mark Twain had earlier remarked, in *A Tramp Abroad* (1880): 'The Cross of the Legion of Honour has been conferred upon me. However, few escape that distinction.'

A delectable gal from Augusta
vowed that nobody ever had bussed her.
But an expert from France
took a bilingual chance
and the mixture of tongues quite nonplussed her.

Conrad Aiken, *A Seizure of Limericks* (1965)

Liberté! Fraternité! Sexualité!

Graffito in Paris, 1980s

I have heard some say ... [homosexual] practices are allowed in France and in other NATO countries. We are not French, and we are not other nationals. We are British, thank God!

Lord Montgomery of Alamein, speaking in the House of Lords, 24 May 1965, on the second reading of the Sexual Offences Bill

Their Insolent and Unfounded Airs of Superiority

I do not dislike the French from the vulgar antipathy between neighbouring nations, but for their insolent and unfounded airs of superiority.

Horace Walpole, letter to Hannah Moore, 14 October 1787. So that's all right then.

A Frenchman must be always talking, whether he knows anything of the matter or not.

Samuel Johnson, quoted in James Boswell, *Life of Samuel Johnson* (1791)

The Frenchman feels an easy mastery in speaking his mother tongue, and attributes it to some native superiority of parts that lifts him high above us barbarians of the West.

J.R. Lowell (1819–91), 'On a Certain Condescension in Foreigners'

But there's always something fishy about the French!
Whether Prince or Politician
We've a sinister suspicion
That behind their *savoir-faire*
They share
A common contempt
For every mother's son of us.

Noël Coward, 'There's Always Something Fishy about the French', song from *Conversation Piece* (1934)

The French are tremendous snobs, despite that rather showy and ostentatious Revolution.

Arthur Marshall

Governing a Country with 246 Varieties of Cheese

How can you govern a country which has 246 varieties of cheese?

Charles de Gaulle, quoted in Ernest Mignon, *Les Mots du Général* (1962). De Gaulle made this observation in 1951, complaining: 'One can only unite the French under the threat of danger.' Incidentally, in an article on the future written in 1984, *National Lampoon* predicted that in 2013 the French will have established 'cheese as the universal currency'.

If it were not for the government, we should have nothing left to laugh at in France.
Nicolas-Sébastien Chamfort (1740–94)

The simple thing is to consider the French as an erratic and brilliant people ... who have all the gifts except that of running their country.
James Cameron, in the *News Chronicle*, 1954

A small acquaintance with history shows that all Governments are selfish and the French Governments more selfish than most.
Lord Eccles

France is an absolute monarchy, tempered by songs.
Nicolas-Sébastien Chamfort, *Characters and Anecdotes* (1795)

The British, having had their Glorious Revolution in 1688 and achieved a constitutional monarchy, generally abhorred French absolutism:

France was long a despotism tempered by epigrams.
Thomas Carlyle, *History of the French Revolution* (1837)

If the French noblesse had been capable of playing cricket with their peasants, their chateaux would never have been burnt.
G.M. Trevelyan, *English Social History* (1942)

The French Revolution itself filled many a Briton with horror:
In the groves of their academy, at the end of every vista, you see nothing but the gallows.
Edmund Burke, *Reflections on the Revolution in France* (1790)

A nation grown free in a single day is a child born with the limbs and the vigour of a man, who would take a drawn sword for his rattle, and set the house in a blaze that he might chuckle over the splendour.
Sydney Smith, quoted in Hesketh Pearson, *The Smith of Smiths* (1934)

I think perhaps we manage our revolutions much more quietly in this country.
Margaret Thatcher, quoted in the *Daily Telegraph*, 12 July 1989, following the bicentenary celebrations of the Revolution in France

In the wake of the Revolution came the Directory, which ruled France from 1795 until Napoleon's coup of 1799:
A system of tyranny, the most galling, the most horrible, the most undisguised in all its parts and attributes that has stained the page of history or disgraced the annals of the world.
William Pitt the Younger, speech in the House of Commons, 10 November 1797

Of France today:
Corruption oozes from its body politic.
Stuart Jeffries, in the *Observer*, 28 January 2001

Serving Up Shit: The Arts in France

The French bourgeois doesn't dislike shit, provided it is served up to him at the right time.

Jean-Paul Sartre, *Saint Genet: Actor and Martyr* (1952)

Reminding one of William Hogarth's description of French architecture:

All gilt and beshit.

The sickly cultural pathos which the whole of France indulges in, that fetishism of the cultural heritage.

Jean Baudrillard, *America* (1986)

France, famed in all great arts, in none supreme.

Matthew Arnold, 'To a Republican Friend – continued' (1849)

One of the problems might be that ...

The French don't say what they mean, don't read as they write, and don't sing according to the notes.

Italian saying

French music has not been to everyone's taste:

I believe I have demonstrated that there is neither rhythm nor melody in French music ... that French singing is endless squawking, unbearable to the unbiased ear ... And so I deduce that the French have no music and cannot have any music – and if they ever have, more's the pity for them.

Jean-Jacques Rousseau, *Lettre sur la musique française* (1753)

And when it comes to [French] singers and songstresses – they ought never to be called that – for they do not sing, but shriek, howl, and that full-throatedly, through nose and gullet.

Wolfgang Amadeus Mozart, letter, 1778

French painters have similarly come in for attack:

Although I had been informed that the present French artists were low in merit, I did not expect to find them, with little exception, so totally devoid of it.

Thomas Cole, Journal, 1831

Since Matisse French painting has hardly been noted for ... anything much beyond tricksiness and etiolated chic ... The awfulness of latter-day French mannerisms, the second-hand novelties, the Swingles-Singers-style tepid abstractions ...

William Feaver, in the *Observer*, 1985

French literature has also had its admirers:

Literature has become consumptive. It spits and slobbers, covers its blisters with salve and sticking-plaster, and has grown bald from too much hair-slicking. It would take Christs of art to cure this leper.

Gustave Flaubert, letter to Louis Boulhet, 1850. This tirade was inspired by a reading of Eugène Sue's *Arthur*.

The production of obscurity in Paris compares to the production of motor cars in Detroit in the great period of American industry.

Ernest Gellner, on BBC TV's *The Late Show*, 15 October 1992

Everything is a Pretext for a Good Dinner

Everything ends this way in France – everything. Weddings, christenings, duels, burials, swindlings, diplomatic affairs – everything is a pretext for a good dinner.

Jean Anouilh, *Cécile* (1949)

French films follow a basic formula: Husband sleeps with Jeanne because Bernadette cuckolded him by sleeping with Christophe, and in the end they all go off to a restaurant.

Sophie Marceau, quoted in the *Observer*, 26 March 1995

Lunch kills half of Paris, supper the other half.

Montesquieu (1689–1755), *Variétés*

French food was not always admired, especially when the British were going through one of their periodic bouts of Francophobia. When such was the case, French food was definitely unwholesome and unmanly:

As to the repast, it was made up of a parcel of kickshaws, contrived by a French cook, without one substantial article adapted to the satisfaction of an English appetite. The pottage was little better than bread soaked in dish washings, luke-warm. The ragouts looked as if they had been once eaten and half digested: the fricassees were involved in a nasty yellow poultice; and the rotis were scorched and stinking, for the honour of the fumet. The dessert consisted of faded fruit and iced froth, a good emblem of our landlady's character; the

table-beer was sour, the water foul, and the wine vapid.

Tobias Smollett, *The Expedition of Humphry Clinker* (1771)

There is nothing so vile or repugnant to nature, but you may plead prescription for it, in the customs of some nation or other. A Parisian likes mortified flesh ...

Tobias Smollett, *Travels through France and Italy* (1766)

... famed as the French always are for ragouts,
No creature can tell what they put in their stews,
Whether bull-frogs, old gloves, or old wigs, or old shoes.

R.H. Barham, *Ingoldsby Legends*, 'The Bagman's Dog' (1840–47)

Housewarming at Zola's. Very tasty dinner, including some grouse whose scented flesh Daudet compared to an old courtesan's flesh marinated in a bidet.

Edmond de Goncourt, *Journal*, 3 April 1878

Cold Chalk Soup and Alum Cordial

Wine is the other great French achievement:

So closely resembling a blend of cold chalk soup and alum cordial with an additive or two to bring it to the colour of children's pee.

Kingsley Amis, *The Green Man* (1969), describing white burgundies

The friendship of the French is like their wine – exquisite, but of short duration.

German saying

Gluttons for Gastropods

I saw a sign in a French restaurant:
SPECIAL TODAY: NO SNAILS.

Gerard Hoffnung

Racial characteristics: **sawed-off cissies who eat**
snails and slugs and cheese that smells like
people's feet ...

P.J. O'Rourke, 'Foreigners Around the World', in *National*
Lampoon, 1976

Snails. I find this a somewhat disturbing dish, but
the sauce is divine. What I do is order escargots,
and tell them to 'hold' the snails.

Miss Piggy, *Miss Piggy's Guide to Life (As Told to Henry*
Beard) (1981)

A bad liver is to a Frenchman what a nervous
breakdown is to an American. Everyone has had one
and everyone wants to talk about it.

Art Buchwald, in the *New York Herald Tribune*, 16 January 1958

The French ...
Utter cowards who force their own children to drink
wine ...

P.J. O'Rourke, 'Foreigners Around the World', in *National*
Lampoon, 1976

France is the largest country in Europe, a great boon for drunks, who need room to fall ...
Alan Coren, *The Sanity Inspector* (1974)

The French drink to get loosened up for an event, to celebrate an event, and even to recover from an event.
Geneviève Guérin, French Commission on Alcoholism, 1980

Pissoirs and Squats

French sanitary arrangements have often made Anglo-Saxon visitors squirm.

In France one must adapt oneself to the fragrance of a urinal.
Gertrude Stein, quoted in Prokosch, *Voices: A Memoir* (1983). Stein commented to Prokosch that 'Alice [B. Toklas] deplores the public urinals ... I keep explaining to Alice that the Parisians are all wine-drinkers and for a gentleman the bladder is more restless than for a lady.'

In addition to the immodesty of the now defunct public pissoirs (where only that portion of the urinator between mid-back and knee was concealed from the gaze of passers-by), the Anglo-Saxon visitor is also faced with the 'squatter', not to mention other technical difficulties of a lavatorial nature ...
France is a country where the money falls apart in your hands and you can't tear the toilet paper.
Billy Wilder

Don't Let's be Beastly to the Germans

Boches, Jerries and Huns

Few peoples have a greater number of insulting monikers than the Germans, many of them perpetuated in generations of war comics.

The quaint old *Boches*, originating early in the 20th century, comes from the French *Alboche*, itself from *Allemand*, German. *Huns* came directly from a speech made by Kaiser Wilhelm II in 1900 to German troops setting off for China to quell the Boxer rising:

No quarter will be given, no prisoners will be taken. Let all who fall into your hands be at your mercy. Just as the Huns a thousand years ago ... gained a reputation in virtue of which they still live in historical tradition, so may the name of Germany become known in ... China that no Chinaman will ever again even dare to look askance at a German.

Jerries is just short for 'Germans', while *Krauts* comes from sauerkraut. Then there's *Fritzes* and *Heinies* (from the first name Heinz), *Cabbage-eaters*, *Beerheads* and *Hop-heads*, *Flatheads* and *Squareheads*, and the more recent *Panzer-heads*.

In the USA in the 19th century, German immigrants were, confusingly, called *Dutch* (from *Deutsch*) – as in the nasty little jingle:

The Irish, the Irish,
They don't amount to much,
But they're all a darn sight better
Than the dirty, dirty Dutch.

But …

Don't Let's be Beastly to the Germans
Noël Coward, title of song

At least, not too much …

Two World Wars and one World Cup, doodah, doodah!
English football song

… the floppy stodginess so often found among the beer-drinking subjects of the Kaiser …
Captain F.S. Brereton, *With French at the Front* (1915)

EIGHTH ARMY PUSHES BOTTLE UP GERMANS
Daily Express headline, 1942 (possibly apocryphal)

The Hun is always either at your throat or at your feet.
Winston Churchill, speech to the US Congress, 19 May 1943

Racial characteristics: piggish-looking sadomasochistic automatons whose only known forms of relaxation are swilling watery beer from vast tubs and singing the idiotically repetitive verses of their porcine folk tunes … Their language lacks any semblance of civilized speech. Their

usual diet consists almost wholly of old cabbage and sections of animal intestines filled with blood and gore.
P.J. O'Rourke, 'Foreigners Around the World', in *National Lampoon*, 1976

This is all a German racket designed to take over the whole of Europe. It has to be thwarted. This rushed take-over by the Germans on the worst possible basis, with the French behaving like poodles to the Germans, is absolutely intolerable.
Nicholas Ridley on the European Community, interviewed in the *Spectator*, 14 July 1990. Ridley was obliged to resign as Margaret Thatcher's Secretary for Trade and Industry shortly after making these remarks, which he thought were off the record.

The British motor industry is really owned by Nazis.
Jeremy Clarkson, BBC motoring correspondent, quips at the National Motor Show, 1998

... admit it, we all hate them.
A.A. Gill, 1999

I Wish the Germans were Frogs

The Germans have over the centuries earned the enmity of many European peoples:

The French ...
I wish I were a stork and the Germans were frogs in the marshes, so I could devour them all; or else a pike in a lake and they fish, so I could eat them this way.
Pope Martin IV (originally Simon de Brion), in *c.* 1284

Let's Blitz Fritz!

Help our boys clout the Krauts.
The *Sun*, before England's World Cup semi-final
against Germany, 1990

**We beat them in '45, we beat them in '66,
now for the battle of '90.**
The *Sun*, 1990

**If their football was as bad as their sense of
humour they wouldn't be in the World Cup.**
Bernard Manning, 1990

LET'S BLITZ FRITZ!
The *Sun*, 17 June 1996, when England played
Germany during the European championship, held
in England. Only nine days earlier the paper had
urged its readers to 'Treat our European guests with
respect and affection.'

HUN-NIL
The *Sunday People* greets England's 1–0 defeat of
Germany in the 2000 European championship.

DON'T MENTION THE SCORE!
Headlines in the *News of the World* and the
Independent on Sunday greet England's 5–1 defeat
of Germany in a vital World Cup qualifying game, 1
September 2001.

The Italians ...
Wherever Germans are, it is unhealthy for Italians.
Italian saying

I should be pleased, I suppose, that Hitler has carried out a revolution on our lines. But they are Germans. So they will end by ruining our idea.
Benito Mussolini

The Austrians ...
The only way to treat a Prussian is to step on his toes until he apologizes.
Austrian proverb

The Russians ...
The godless Germans.
Ivan the Terrible, letter to Prince Kurbsky, September 1577

If anyone is born a German, God has sufficiently punished him already.
Russian saying

The German may be a good fellow, but it is best to hang him just the same.
Russian saying

The Danes ...
Rather die with Denmark than rot with Prussia.
Danish saying

The Croats ...
Better Turkish hatred than German love.
Croatian saying

Even the obscure Ruthenians …
Marry a German and you'll see that the women have hairy tongues.
Ruthenian saying

Poles on the Germans

One German a beer; two Germans an organization; three Germans a war.

The German is as sly as the plague.

A dead German, a dead dog; the difference is but slight.

The German may be as big as a poplar tree, but he is stupid as a bean.

Even if he tempts no one else, the devil will persuade the German.

**Serve the German with all your heart;
Your reward will be a fart.**

Peace with the German is like a wolf and a sheep living together.

As the Germans themselves used to say:
**With the Germans friendship make,
But as neighbours do not take.**

The National Industry

War is Prussia's national industry.
Comte Mirabeau (1749–91), attributed remark

When they are not at war they do a little hunting, but spend most of their time in idleness, sleeping and eating. The strongest and most warlike do nothing. They vegetate ...
Tacitus, *Germania* (AD 1st–2nd century)

The history of Germany is a history of ... the licentiousness of the strong, and the oppression of the weak ... of general imbecility, confusion, and misery.
Alexander Hamilton, in *The Federalist* (1787–8)

German military muscle has at times been underestimated:
All military men who have seen the Prussian army at its annual reviews of late years will have unequivocally declared that France would walk all over it and get without difficulty to Berlin.
Lord Palmerston, when prime minister in 1863. Paris surrendered to the Prussians on 28 January 1871.

Prussia is a country without any bottom, and in my opinion could not maintain a war for six weeks.
Benjamin Disraeli, remark in 1864. That year Prussia beat Denmark, and two years later it defeated Austria – in seven weeks.

I will tear up the Boches within two months.
Joseph Joffre, commander-in-chief of the French army, in November 1914

Germany has reduced savagery to a science, and this great war for the victorious peace of justice must go on until the German cancer is cut clean out of the world body.

Theodore Roosevelt, speech, 30 September 1917

One thing I will say for the Germans – they are always perfectly willing to give somebody's land to somebody else.

Will Rogers

Here Comes the Master Race!

Springtime for Hitler and Germany,
Deutschland is happy and gay.
We're marching to a faster pace,
Look out, here comes the Master Race! ...
Don't be stupid, be a smarty
Come and join the Nazi party!

Lyric from cod-musical *Springtime for Hitler*, in the film *The Producers* (1967), written by Mel Brooks

A monstrous tyranny, never surpassed in the dark, lamentable catalogue of human crime.

Winston Churchill, speech to the House of Commons, 13 May 1940

Hitler
Has only got one ball!
Goering
Has two, but very small!

Himmler
Has something similar,
But poor old Goebbels
Has no balls at all!

Anonymous World War II song

East or West …

I love Germany so dearly that I hope there will always be two of them.
François Mauriac (1885–1970), French novelist

They came, they saw, they did a little shopping.
Graffito on the Berlin Wall, December 1989, after thousands of East Berliners flooded into West Berlin

The East German manages to combine a Teutonic capacity for bureaucracy with a Russian capacity for infinite delay.
Goronwy Rees

West Germans are tall, pert and orthodontically corrected, with hands, teeth and hair as clean as their clothes and clothes as sharp as their looks. Except for the fact that they all speak English pretty well, they're indistinguishable from Americans.
P.J. O'Rourke, 'The Death of Communism', in *Rolling Stone*, November 1989

It's like the Beatles coming together again – let's hope they don't go on a world tour.
Matt Frei, in 1990, on German reunification

In politics, as in grammar, one should be able to tell
the substantives from adjectives. Hitler was
substantive; Mussolini only an adjective. Hitler was a
nuisance; Mussolini was bloody. Together a bloody
nuisance.

Salvador de Madariaga (1886–1978), Spanish historian and
diplomat

If Hitler invaded hell I would make at least a favourable
reference to the devil in the House of Commons.

Winston Churchill, *The Second World War* (1950)

An Orderly and Insensitive People

The German people are an orderly, vain, deeply
sentimental and rather insensitive people. They seem
to feel at their best when they are singing in chorus,
saluting or obeying orders.

H.G. Wells, *Travels of a Republican Radical in Search of Hot
Water* (1939)

I can think of no people more dismembered than the
Germans. You see workmen but no human beings,
thinkers but no human beings, priests but no human
beings, masters and servants, youths and staid people,
but no human beings.

Friedrich Hölderlin, *Hyperion* (1799)

A German is someone who cannot tell a lie without
believing it himself.

Theodor Adorno (1903–69), German philosopher, *Minima
Memorialia*

A German film-goer was beaten to death in a Bonn cinema by ushers because he had brought his own popcorn.
Karl Shaw

I asked him, 'Are you a pole vaulter?' He said, 'No, I'm a German and how did you know my name was Walter?'
Billy Connolly

Appallingly Thorough

How appallingly thorough these Germans always managed to be, how emphatic! In sex no less than war – in scholarship, in science. Diving deeper than anyone else and coming up muddier.
Aldous Huxley, *Time Must Have a Stop* (1944)

The German – as opposed to the human – mind.
William James (1842–1910), American philosopher and psychologist

The German mind has a talent for making no mistakes but the very greatest.
Clifton Fadiman

The Bavarian unites the discipline of the Austrian with the charm of the Prussian.
Werner Heisenberg (1901–76), Bavarian physicist

Ponderous, Viscous and Clumsy: German Culture

Everything ponderous, viscous, and pompously clumsy, all long-winded and wearying species of style are developed in profuse variety among Germans.
Friedrich Nietzsche, *Beyond Good and Evil* (1886)

The Germans are like women, you can scarcely ever fathom their depths – they haven't any.
Friedrich Nietzsche, *The Antichrist* (1888)

A German singer! I should as soon expect to get pleasure from the neighing of my horse.
Frederick the Great (1712–86), king of Prussia

The Germans (which I am ashamed to utter) do howl like wolves.
Andreas Ornithoparcus, *Andreas Ornithoparcus His Micrologus* (trans. John Dowland, 1609)

On German composers:
They are not of our temperament, they are so heavy, and lack clarity.
Claude Debussy, quoted by Nadezdha von Meck in a letter to Tchaikovsky, 1880

The great majority of Germans, realizing the impossibility of talking their language with any degree of success, abandon it altogether, and communicate with one another on brass bands. German sounds better on a band, but not much.
Frank Richardson, *Love, and All About It* (1907)

It should have been written into the armistice treaty that the Germans would be required to lay down their accordions along with their arms.

Bill Bryson

Hitler, there was a painter! He could paint an entire apartment in one afternoon. Two coats!

Line from the film *The Producers* (1967), written by Mel Brooks

The Most Extravagantly Ugly Language

German is the most extravagantly ugly language. It sounds like someone using a sick-bag on a 747.

William Rushton, *Holiday Inn, Ghent* (1984)

Life is too short to learn German.

Richard Porson (1759–1808), British classical scholar

They say ve for we, and wisy wersy.

Thomas Hood (1799–1845), British poet, 'Up the Rhine'

A frightful dialect for the stupid, the pedant and dullard sort.

Thomas Carlyle, *History of Frederick II* (1858–65)

[The German language] was developed solely to afford the speaker the opportunity to spit at strangers under the guise of polite conversation.

The National Lampoon Encyclopedia of Humor (1973)

I speak Spanish to God, Italian to women, French to men – and German to my horse.

Charles V (1500–1558), Holy Roman Emperor

A Verb in His Mouth

Mark Twain had a lot to say about the German language. As he once remarked:

I can *understand* German as well as the maniac that invented it, but I *talk* it best through an interpreter.

And,

Whenever the literary German dives into a sentence, that is the last you are going to see of him till he emerges on the other side of his Atlantic with his verb in his mouth.

A Connecticut Yankee in King Arthur's Court (1889)

I heard a Californian student in Heidelberg say, in one of his calmest moods, that he would rather decline two drinks than one German adjective.

A Tramp Abroad (1880)

A verb has a hard enough time of it in this world when it's all together. It's downright inhuman to split it up. But that's just what those Germans do. They take part of a verb and put it down here, like a stake, and they take the other part of it and put away over yonder like another stake, and between those two limits they just shovel in German.

Speech, New York, 1900

Whatever music sounds like, I am glad to say that it does not sound in the smallest degree like German.

Oscar Wilde, 'The Critic As Artist' (1890)

Gorging and Swilling

The Germans gorge and swill themselves to poverty and hell.

German saying

The Prussians have two stomachs and no heart.

German saying

Think of the man who first tried German sausage.

Jerome K. Jerome, *Three Men in a Boat* (1889)

This nation has arbitrarily stupefied itself for nearly a thousand years: nowhere have the two great European narcotics, alcohol and Christianity, been more wickedly misused ... How much moody heaviness, lameness, humidity, and dressing-gown mood, how much beer is in German intelligence!

Friedrich Nietzsche, *Twilight of the Idols* (1889)

A German doesn't need to jump into the water; he can swill to death in a glass of beer or wine.

German saying

The Germans are exceedingly fond of Rhine wines; they are put up in tall, slender bottles, and are considered a pleasant beverage. One tells them from vinegar by the label.

Mark Twain, *A Tramp Abroad* (1880)

Three things are in a poor plight: birds in the hands of children, young girls in the hands of old men, and wine in the hands of Germans.
Italian saying

They are a fine people but quick to catch the disease of anti-humanity. I think it's because of their poor elimination. Germany is a headquarters for constipation.
George Grosz (1893–1959), German artist

After all that gorging and swilling, the Germans go to the spa to make themselves feel better. In the baths they are joined by valetudinarians from around the world:
Germany, the diseased world's bathhouse.
Mark Twain, *Autobiography*

The Boors of Europe

The Germans since 1870 have taken the place of the English as the boors of Europe.
Price Collier, *England and the English* (1909)

You must not scratch your throat whilst you eat, with the bare hand. But if it happens that you cannot help scratching, then courteously take a portion of your dress, and scratch with that.
Tannhäusser (14th century), advice on table manners

Send the pig to Saxonland, wash it with soap; the hog returns and remains a hog.
Estonian saying

Benelux Sucks:
The Lowest of Low Countries

Dike Jumpers and Cloggites:
Holland and the Dutch

Other terms for the Dutch include *Butterbags* and *Frogs* – the latter dating from the 17th century, when England was often at war with the Dutch. When France became Britain's number-one enemy in the 18th century, the epithet was transferred.

Arising from the Anglo-Dutch Wars, *Dutch* became a derogatory stereotype, implying hard-drinking, stolid and stodgy, gruff, grumpy and generally mean. The following phrases all derive from some aspect of this image.

Drinking: *Dutch courage*, temporary bravery induced by alcohol; *Dutch feast*, one where the host gets drunk before the guests.

Enumerating eight types of drunkenness, one 16th-century commentator identified the eighth as

Fox drunke, when he is craftie and cunning, as manie of the Dutchmen bee.

Thomas Nashe, *Pierce Penniless* (1592)

Shakespeare also noted the Dutch potency in 'potting', and spoke of

Your swag-bellied Hollander.

Othello, II.iii

Meanness: *Dutch fuck*, meaning (a) lighting one cigarette from another, so saving matches, (b) intercourse between the breasts (presumably cheaper, if paid for); *Dutch auction*, a sale where the 'reductions' are illusory; *Dutch bargain*, a one-sided bargain; *Dutch gold*, an alloy of copper and zinc, used for gilding; *to go Dutch*, to share the price of a meal, which would thus be a *Dutch treat*.

Dourness: *Dutch comfort*, saying 'Just think, it could be worse'; *Dutch uncle*, one who lectures severely and critically, laying down the law.

All hail the Dutch, long-suffering neutrons in the endless movement against oppression and exploitation. Let us hear it for the Dutch, bland and obliging victims of innumerable wars which have rendered their land as flat as their treats ... Every one of them is an uncle, not a one can muster real courage ... All hail the Dutch, nonpeople in the people's war!
Tony Hendra, 'EEC! It's the US of E!', in *National Lampoon*, 1976

Compared with Greece and Italy, Holland is but a platter-faced cold-gin-and-water country, after all, and a heavy, barge-built, web-footed race are its inhabitants.
Sir Francis Bond Head (1793–1875)

A dark German, a fair Italian, and a red Spaniard seldom bode good, as does a Dutchman of any colour.
German saying

Like the Germans, the Dutch fall into two quite distinct physical types: the small, corpulent, red-faced Edams, and the thinner, paler, larger Goudas.

Alan Coren, *The Sanity Inspector* (1974)

Apart from cheese and tulips, the main product of the country is advocaat, a drink made from lawyers.

Alan Coren, *The Sanity Inspector* (1974)

**The indigested vomit of the sea
Fell to the Dutch by just propriety.**

Andrew Marvell, 'The Character of Holland' (*c.* 1664)

Holland ... lies so low they're only saved by being dammed.

Thomas Hood, 'Letter from Martha Penny to Rebecca Page', in *Up the Rhine* (1840)

The Scotch may be compared to a tulip planted in dung, but I never see a Dutchman in his own house, but I think of a magnificent Egyptian Temple dedicated to an ox.

Oliver Goldsmith, letter from Leyden to Rev. Thomas Contarine, 1754

We always like our pop stars to be like Greek gods: bigger, better and uglier than us. We hate the bores, Jesus Christ and the Dutch. Especially the Dutch.

Malcolm McLaren

Amsterdam, Rotterdam, and all the other dams! Damned if I'll go.

King George V

What a po-faced lot these Dutch are.
Prince Philip, during a visit to Amsterdam in 1968

Get out and clog 'em, lads. Go and gut 'em, Gazza!
The *Sun*, 11 June 1996, when England played the
Netherlands during the Euro 96 competition.

A donkey is a horse translated into Dutch.
G.C. Lichtenberg

- -

Dutch Painters

**The patient devotion of besotted lives to
delineation of bricks and fogs, cattle and
ditchwater.**
John Ruskin, *The Stones of Venice* (1851–3)

- -

Belgium: Walloons and Flems

In 1830 five European powers met in London and created
Belgium out of bits of France and the Netherlands.

**Belgium is just a country invented by the British
to annoy the French.**
Charles de Gaulle

The country has long suffered from the mutual hatred of
the Flemish-speakers and the French-speaking Walloons:

That isn't a dog; that's a Fleming.
Walloon saying

Where the Walloons sit, the grass is not green for seven years.
Flemish saying

Belief in progress is a doctrine of idlers and Belgians.
Charles Baudelaire

Belgium is the most densely populated country in Europe ... the land is entirely invisible, except in the small hours of the morning, being for the rest of the time completely under foot ... the sprout was developed by Brussels agronomists, this being the largest cabbage a housewife could possibly carry through the teeming streets.
Alan Coren, *The Sanity Inspector* (1974)

Belgium is known affectionately to the French as 'the gateway to Germany' and just as affectionately to the Germans as 'the gateway to France'.
Tony Hendra, 'EEC! It's the US of E!', in *National Lampoon*, 1976

Lastly, Little Luxemburg

On a clear day, from the terrace ... you can't see Luxemburg at all. This is because a tree is in the way.
Alan Coren, *The Sanity Inspector* (1974)

Spain:
A Stranded Whale

A whale stranded upon the sea shore of Europe.
Edmund Burke, referring to Spain in a speech to the House of Commons

A nation swoln with ignorance and pride ...
The land of war and crimes.
Lord Byron, *Childe Harold's Pilgrimage* (1812–18), Cantos i and ii

Dons and Oil Slicks

The Armada chaps that Drake et al thrashed were known as *Dons*. The Spanish have also been called *Garlic-eaters* ...

The Spaniard, I have heard it said
Eats garlic, by itself, on bread ...
Hilaire Belloc, *On Food*

More recently Spaniards (and also Latin Americans and Italians) have been known by the even more offensive term *Spics* (originating in the USA in the early 20th century), which in turn gave rise to the rhyming slang *Oil Slicks*. 'Spic' is said to come from the phrase 'no spicka da English'; alternatively, it is an abbreviation of *spiggoty*, a mispronunciation of spaghetti.

Singeing the King of Spain's Beard

Thus did cheeky Francis Drake describe his raid on Cadiz in 1587. At that time Catholic Spain was Protestant England's number-one enemy, hence *Spanish gout* became a popular term for venereal disease (later known as the *French pox* when the French took over as number-one beastly foreigners).

All evil comes from Spain; all good from the north.
Sir Thomas Chaloner, letter from Florence, 1597

The English were proud of their victories over the Spaniards, but fearful of the reprisals that the mighty Spanish empire might inflict on them:
Who would therefore repose trust in such a nation of ravenous strangers, and especially in those Spaniards which more greedily thirst after English blood, than after the lives of any other people in Europe, for the many overthrows and dishonours they have received at our hands, whose weakness we have discovered to the world.
Sir Walter Raleigh, report (1591) of the last fight of *The Revenge*

Raleigh *really* didn't like the Spanish:
It were an horrible dishonour to be over reached by any of these dry and subtil headed Spaniards.
Discourse on the marriage of Prince Henry (1611)

One of the great English heroes of this period was Sir Richard Grenville, who died following a battle between his ship, *The Revenge*, and a fleet of 15 Spanish galleons off the Azores in

1591. He had refused to withdraw, which would have meant leaving sick men ashore to the mercy of 'these Inquisition dogs and the devildoms of Spain':

And Sir Richard said again: 'We be all good English men.
Let us bang these dogs of Seville, the children of the
**   devil,**
For I never turned my back upon Don or devil yet.'
Alfred, Lord Tennyson, 'The Revenge' (1878)

Anglo-Spanish enmity these days is largely reserved for the football field:
GIVE 'EM A SPAINKING!
The *Sun*, 13 June 1996, when England played Spain during the Euro 96 competition. Only five days earlier the paper had urged its readers to 'Treat our European guests with respect and affection.'

Braggarts, Snobs and Sticky Fingers

Honour to a Spaniard, no matter how dishonest, is as real a thing as water, wine, or olive oil. There is honour among pickpockets and honour among whores. It is simply that the standards differ.
Ernest Hemingway, *Death in the Afternoon* (1932)

A Spaniard and a braggart are synonymous.
German saying

A Spaniard is no Spaniard if he is not a snob.
German saying

All Spaniards have sticky fingers. In past centuries, the pots on the stove would have padlocks on them.
German saying

An Overflow of Sombreness

Spain is an overflow of sombreness ... a strong and threatening tide of history meets you at the frontier.

Wyndham Lewis, *The Wild Body*, 'A Soldier of Humour' (1927)

The only good that comes from the east is the sun.

Portuguese saying – Spain is to the east of Portugal

The French are wiser than they seem, and the Spaniards seem wiser than they are.

Francis Bacon, *Essays*, 'Of Seeming Wise'

Spain is the only country where death is the national spectacle.

Federico García Lorca, on bull-fighting

A Spaniard is not to be trusted any more than if he had a cartload of earth in his mouth.

German saying

Three Spaniards, four opinions.

Spanish saying

The Spaniard is a bad servant, but a worse master.

Thomas Adams, *Sermons* (1629), possibly quoting an existing English saying

Spain would be a fine country, if there were no Spaniards in it.
German saying

The Spaniards are like body lice; once they are there it is not easy to get rid of them.
German saying

The Costa del Crime: Tourists' Spain

The Costa del Sol ... is particularly famous across Europe for being a place for criminals and karaoke performers to escape justice.
Tim Dedopulos, *The Best Book of Insults and Putdowns Ever!* (1998)

A country that has sold its soul for cement and petrol, and can only be saved by a series of earthquakes.
Cyril Connolly

There is never any doubt, then, that one has arrived in Spain ... There is a faint sound of drums, a smell of crude olive oil, and a current of strong, leaking electricity.
Anthony Carson, *A Train to Tarragona* (1957)

Sulphurous Urination:
Spanish Wine and Food

The Spanish wine, my God, it is foul, catpiss is champagne compared, this is the sulphurous urination of some aged horse.

D.H. Lawrence, letter from Palma to Rhys Davis, 25 April 1929

Keep clear of wine, I tell you, white or red,
Especially Spanish wines ...

Geoffrey Chaucer, 'The Pardoner's Tale' (trans. Nevill Coghill)

In a Spanish inn, you will find only what you have brought there yourself.

French saying

He who would eat in Spain must bring his kitchen along.

German saying

The meal was of course filthy. It began with glazed seafood and continued with ridiculously tough veal or something, the whole washed down with vile wine. Spanish food and drink were never up to much in my experience, but you used to be able to depend on simplicities like tomatoes, onions, olives, oranges and the local red. Not now. The bread has gone too. The only things that are always all right are potatoes, tinned fruit, ice cream and sherry. And Coca Cola, I dare say.

Kingsley Amis, 'Amis Abroad', in the *Spectator*, 23 November 1963

Moving west over the border one may fare no better, as an 18th-century traveller complained:

The Portuguese had need have the stomach of ostriches to digest the loads of greasy victuals with which they cram themselves. Their vegetables, their rice, their poultry are all stewed in the essence of ham and so strongly seasoned with pepper and spices that a spoonful of pease ... is sufficient to set one's mouth in a flame.

William Beckford, *Italy: with Sketches of Spain and Portugal* (1834)

Italy:
A Paradise of Devils

Italy is a paradise inhabited by devils.
German saying, quoted by Sir Henry Wotton (1568–1639),
Letters from Italy

Italy might well be called a paradise; for whoever gets there readily falls into sin.
German saying

There are *two* Italies ... The one is the most sublime and lovely contemplation that can be conceived by the imagination of man; the other is the most degraded, disgusting, and odious. What do you think? Young women of rank actually eat – you will never guess what – *garlick*!
Percy Bysshe Shelley, letter from Naples, 22 December 1818

Wops and Eyties, Macaronis and Meatballs

The derogatory slang *Wops* for Italians originated in the 19th century, and derives from the Spanish word *guapo*, meaning a dandy. Via rhyming slang, Wops has become *Grocer's Shops*. *Eyties* or *I-Ties* first appeared in the 1920s, in the USA; the Australian variant is *Eyetos*. A number of other slang terms are culinary in inspiration: *Garlic-eaters* or *Garlic-snappers*, *Icecreamers*, *Spaghetti-benders*, *Macaronis* and *Meatballs*.

The median Italian ... is a cowardly baritone who consumes 78.3 kilometres of carbohydrates a month and drives about in a car slightly smaller than he is, looking for a divorce.

Alan Coren, *The Sanity Inspector* (1974)

Venice – Streets Full of Water

Streets full of water. Please advise.

Robert Benchley (1889–1945), telegram to his editor at the *New Yorker* on arriving in Venice

The most striking thing about the City of Venice is the complete absence of the smell of horse dung.

Alphonse Allais (1854–1905), French humorist

Venice is like eating an entire box of chocolate liqueurs at one go.

Truman Capote, quoted in the *Observer*, 1961

The 'cowardly' stereotype of Italian manhood presumably originates in the Desert War of 1941–3, when the Italians, very sensibly, did a lot of retreating and surrendering. This has inspired innumerable jokes, for example:

Q: How many gears does an Italian tank have?
A: One forward, four reverse.

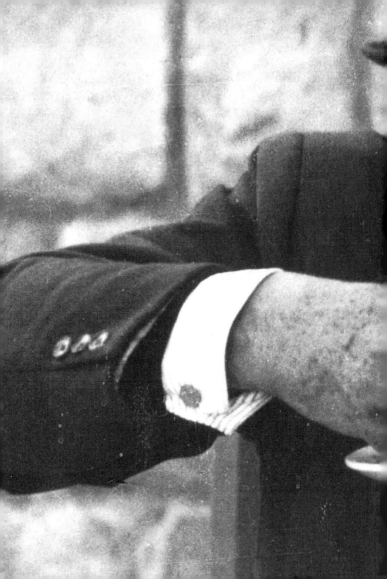

The Italians' technological contribution to mankind stopped with the pizza oven.
Bill Bryson

HSIR: High Speed Italian Rust
Title of website devoted to Italian cars

Italy is the paradise of the flesh, the hell of the soul, the purgatory of the pocketbook.
German saying

England is a paradise for women, and hell for horses: Italy a paradise for horses, hell for women …
Robert Burton, *The Anatomy of Melancholy* (1621)

Half an Italian is one too many in the house.
French and German saying

All Italians are plunderers.
Napoleon Bonaparte, remark, to which a lady present wittily replied, '*Non tutti, ma buona parte*' ('not all, but a good part')

The Italian will kill his father for money.
Illyrian saying

Q: **How do you tell the Italians at a cock fight?**
A: **They're the ones betting on the duck.**
Q: **And how can you tell if the Mafia's involved?**
A: **The duck wins.**
Internet joke

I would love to speak Italian but I can't, so I grew underarm hair instead.
Sue Kolinsky

Pouring Themselves over Each Other

Outsiders have often been shocked by what they see as Italian emotional extremism. Some think the Italians to be over-physical ...

And that is ... how they are. So terribly physically all over one another. They pour themselves one over the other like so much melted butter over parsnips.

D.H. Lawrence, *Sea and Sardinia* (1923), referring to the Sicilians in particular

Or otherwise over-excitable ...

In Italy, the whole country is a theatre and the worst actors are on the stage.

George Bernard Shaw

No Law or Government at All

There is, in fact, no law or government at all; and it is wonderful how well things go on without them.

Lord Byron, letter to Thomas Moore, 2 January 1821

Ah, slavish Italy! thou inn of grief!
Vessel without pilot in loud storm!
Lady no longer of fair provinces,
But brothel-house impure!

Dante, *Purgatorio*, Canto vi

Italy is a geographical expression.
Prince Metternich, letter to Lord Palmerston, 6 August 1847

Since World War II, Italy has managed, with characteristic artistry, to create a society that combines a number of the least appealing aspects of socialism with practically all the vices of capitalism.
Gore Vidal, 'Sciasci's Italy' (1979), in *The Second American Revolution* (1982)

Italy is a poor country full of rich people.
Richard Gardner, former US ambassador to Italy, quoted in the *Observer*, 1981

Goats in Rancid Oil: Italian Food

In Italy, the traveller notes
With great disgust the flesh of goats
Appearing on the table d'hotes;
And even this the natives spoil
By frying it in rancid oil.
Hilaire Belloc, *On Food*

macaroni, **n. An Italian food made in the form of a slender, hollow tube. It consists of two parts – the tubing and the hole, the latter being the part that digests.**
Ambrose Bierce, *The Devil's Dictionary* (1906)

Rome – the Eternal City?

If there be a hell, Rome is built over it.
German saying

Radix
Omnia
Malorum et
Avarica
Medieval acrostic: 'ROMA: the root for all things evil and avaricious'

An ass in Germany is a professor in Rome.
German saying

She said that all the sites in Rome were called after London cinemas.
Nancy Mitford, *Pigeon Pie* (1940)

Nobody in Rome works and if it rains in Rome *and* they happen to notice it they blame it on Milan. In Rome people spend most of their time having lunch. And they do it very well – Rome is unquestionably the lunch capital of the world.
Fran Lebowitz, *Metropolitan Life* (1978)

Rome reminds me of a man who lives by exhibiting to travellers his grandmother's corpse.
James Joyce

Viallis, Vieiras and Viagras: Italian Football

I hope Tony Adams is playing because he's the only name I know. All these Viallis, Vieiras and Viagras.
Jack Hayward, chairman of Wolverhampton Wanderers, in 1999, on the number of foreign players involved in a forthcoming match with Arsenal

We played the Italians at their own game. They are very good at diving, cheating, trying to waste time.
Paul Gascoigne, following England's draw against Italy in a World Cup qualifying match, 1997

When Italians tell me it's pasta I check under the sauce to make sure it is. They're masters of the smokescreen. They come out with the 'English are so strong, we're terrible in the air, we can't do this, we can't do that'. Then they beat you 3–0.
Alex Ferguson, manager of Manchester United, just before the club's match against Inter Milan, 1999

Lump the Whole Thing! Italian Art

Lump the whole thing! Say that the Creator made Italy from designs by Michael Angelo!
Mark Twain, *The Innocents Abroad* (1869)

I am damnably sick of Italy, Italian and Italians, outrageously, illogically sick ... I hate to think that

Italians ever did anything in the way of art ... What did they do but illustrate a page or so of the New Testament!

James Joyce, letter to his brother from Rome, 7 December 1906

The Italians say give me a true outline and you may fill it up with turd.

Charles Wilson Peale (1741–1827), US painter

Have you seen that bloody Leonardo da Vinci cartoon? I couldn't see the bloody joke ... The sense of humour must have changed over the years. I bet when that da Vinci cartoon first came out, I bet people were killing themselves. I bet old da Vinci had an accident when he done it ... Apart from that, Pete, it's a different culture. It's Italian y'see, we don't understand it. For instance, *The Mousetrap* did terribly in Pakistan.

Peter Cook and Dudley Moore, 'Art Gallery' sketch, in BBC TV's *Not Only But Also*, 23 January 1965

They spell it Vinci and pronounce it Vinchy; foreigners always spell better than they pronounce.

Mark Twain, *The Innocents Abroad* (1869)

Debauched Italian Airs: Italian Music

The introduction of 'effeminate' Italian opera into Britain in the early 18th century drew stern criticism:

There was an age, (its memory will last!)
Before Italian airs debauched our taste.

Elijah Fenton, 'An Epistle to Mr Southerne, from Kent, January 28, 1710–11'

Curse on this damn'd Italian pathic mode,
To Sodom and to Hell the ready road.

Henry Carey (?1687–1743), 'A Satire on the Luxury and
Effeminacy of the Age'

An unalterable and unquestioned law of the musical
world required that the German text of French operas
sung by Swedish artists should be translated into
Italian for the clearer understanding of English-
speaking audiences.

Edith Wharton, *The Age of Innocence* (1920)

Opera in English is, in the main, just about as sensible
as baseball in Italian.

H.L. Mencken (1880–1956), US journalist and satirist

There are no pianists in Italy, and if you can only play
the scale of C with both hands you pass for a great
artist.

Georges Bizet, letter, 1858

Greasy Greece

Marbleheads and Fruit Salads

In the 19th century the Greeks were called *Marbleheads*, from their ancient statuary. More modern slang terms include *Dimmos*, from the common Greek first name Demosthenes, and *Bubbles*, which is 1950s rhyming slang from 'bubble and squeak'.

***Racial characteristics*: degenerate, dirty and impoverished descendants of a bunch of la-de-da fruit salads who invented democracy and then forgot how to use it while walking around dressed up like girls.**
P.J. O'Rourke, 'Foreigners Around the World', in *National Lampoon* (1976)

Few things can be less tempting and less dangerous than a Greek woman of the age of thirty.
John Carne

In the USA Greeks are simply known as *Griks*, while Greek immigrants in Australia are referred to as *Zorbas*, from the novel and film *Zorba the Greek*. They are also called *Werris*, which is rhyming slang via Werris Creek, and *Grills*, from the Greek near-monopoly of corner cafés in Australia – hence the internet joke:
Q: Why have the Greeks been banned from international soccer?
A: Every time they get a corner they want to open a café.

Greek associations are rather different for the British holidaymaker:

The weird mixture of smells which together compose the anthology of a Greek holiday under the pines – petrol, garlic, wine and goat.

Lawrence Durrell, *Reflections on a Marine Venus* (1953)

* * *

Parthenon? What Parthenon?

Some foreign visitors have failed to register Greece at all. When asked whether he had visited the Parthenon while on tour in Greece, the American basketball player Shaquille O'Neal replied:

I can't really remember the names of the clubs we went to.

* * *

Sad Relic of Departed Worth

**Fair Greece! sad relic of departed worth! ...
Land of lost gods and godlike men.**

Lord Byron, *Childe Harold's Pilgrimage* (1812–18), Canto ii, stanzas 73 and 85

Many in the 19th century remarked on the decline of 'The glory that *was* Greece' (Edgar Allen Poe's words; our italics), by implication sneering at modern Greece and its inhabitants. More recent commentators have been less indirect:

Third World nations such as the Greeks and Irish ...
Alfred Sherman, in 1990

While Byron and other Hellenophiles were battling for
Greek independence in the 1820s, other Britons were less
sympathetic:
**There never was such a humbug as the Greek affair
altogether. However, thank God it has never cost us
a shilling, and never shall.**
Duke of Wellington, remark, February 1828

Out-Cheated Only by the Devil

**A Russian can be cheated only by a Gypsy, a Gypsy
by a Jew, a Jew by a Greek and a Greek by the Devil.**
Greek saying

Over the centuries Greek merchants built up a reputation for
wiliness – still echoed in the US phrase *Greek trust*, meaning
an absolute lack of trust.

Timeo Danaos et dona ferentes.
I fear the Greeks, even though they bear gifts.
Virgil, *Aeneid*, II, 49

Greeks tell the truth, but only once a year.
Russian saying

Three Turks and three Greeks make six heathens.
Serbian saying

After shaking hands with a Greek count your fingers.
Albanian saying

One Greek can outwit ten Jews.
Bulgarian saying

However, the Greeks appear to be outclassed by a couple of other nationalities:
It takes three Jews to cheat a Greek, three Greeks to cheat a Syrian, and three Syrians to cheat an Armenian.
Levantine saying

Believe a Cretan?

The Cretans are always liars, evil beasts, slow bellies.
Epistle of Paul to Titus, 1: 12. The Cretans had achieved this reputation long before Paul's time: the ancient Greek philosophers enjoyed toying with the question as to what to believe when a Cretan tells you that all Cretans are liars.

The people of Crete unfortunately make more history than they can consume locally.
Saki (H.H. Munro), 'The Jesting of Arlington Stringham'

Monsters of Pride and Self-Glorification

Thus Friedrich Nietzsche described the ancient Greek
philosophers – Pythagoras and Plato in particular.

**Out of all those centuries the Greeks can count seven
sages at the most, and if anyone looks at them more
closely I swear he'll not find so much as a half-wise
man or even a third of a wise man among them.**
Erasmus, *Praise of Folly* (1509)

The Trouble with Cyprus

**Realizing they will never be a world power, the
Cypriots have decided to settle for being a world
nuisance.**
George Mikes. Mikes also observed that every Greek
constitutes his own political party of one.

**If these writings of the Greeks agree with the book of
God, they are useless and need not be preserved; if
they disagree, they are pernicious and ought to be
destroyed.**
Omar, Muslim caliph, on burning the library of Alexandria
in *c.* 641, quoted in Edward Gibbon, *The Decline and Fall
of the Roman Empire* (1776–88)

Similarly, the achievements of the ancient Greeks in art have not pleased everybody:

The great mistake is that of the Greeks, never mind how beautiful it is.

Paul Gauguin, letter to Daniel de Monfried, 1897

The Romans tended to patronize the conquered Greeks, even though they'd borrowed their culture:

Scholar, orator, geometrician, painter, PE instructor, fortune-teller, rope-dancer, physician, magician – the hungry little Greek can do everything: send him off to heaven and he'll go there.

Juvenal, *Satires*, 3

Familiarity with ancient Greek learning was once regarded as the pinnacle of scholarship. But not by everybody:

Too servile a submission to the books and opinions of the ancients has spoiled many an ingenious man, and plagued the world with an abundance of pedants and coxcombs.

James Puckle (?1677–1724)

A man is in general better pleased when he has a good dinner upon his table, than when his wife talks Greek.

Samuel Johnson, quoted in John Hawkins (ed.), *The Works of Samuel Johnson* (1787)

Russia: Land of the Bully Bear

The term *Bear* for a Russian dates from the early 19th century. *Russkis* or *Rooskies* arrived a century later. In America in the 19th century, Russians were known as *Cabbage-eaters*.

Drunken Lard-Bags

Ivan Yakovlevich, like any honest Russian working man, was a terrible drunkard.
Nikolai Gogol, 'The Nose' (1836)

***Racial characteristics*: brutish, dumpy, boorish lard-bags in cardboard double-breasted suits. Lickspittle slaveys to the maniacal schemes of their blood-lusting Red overlords. They make bicycles out of cement and can be sent to Siberia for listening to the wrong radio station.**
P.J. O'Rourke, 'Foreigners Around the World', in *National Lampoon*, 1976

A nation of sheep. Angry sheep, but nevertheless sheep, and in sheep's clothing.
James Kirkup (1918–), British poet and travel writer

Ivan was coming with us only as far as Minsk where he was attending a village idiots' conference. The banners read 'Welcome Idiots'.
Woody Allen

The Bear That Walks Like a Man

Make ye no truce with Adam-zad, the bear that walks like a man.
Rudyard Kipling

Scratch the Russian and you will find the Tartar.
Joseph de Maistre (1753–1821), French political philosopher and diplomat. Also attributed to Napoleon and the Prince de Ligne.

The devil you can ban with the cross, but of the Russian you can never get rid.
Ukrainian saying

Be friendly with the Russian, but take care that you have a rock ready on your chest.
Ukrainian saying

Oh, if the Queen were a man, she would like to go and give those Russians, whose word one cannot believe, such a beating! We shall never be friends again till we have it out.
Queen Victoria, letter to Disraeli, 10 January 1878. Britain and Russia were frequently at odds through the 19th century over the 'Eastern Question'.

Let it be clearly understood that the Russian is a delightful person till he tucks in his shirt. As an Oriental he is charming. It is only when he insists on being treated as the most easterly of western peoples instead of the most westerly of easterns

that he becomes a racial anomaly extremely difficult to handle.

Rudyard Kipling, *Life's Handicap*, 'The Man Who Was' (1891)

I cannot go very far with those who dread the Russians ... Their people are unwarlike, their officials corrupt, their rulers only competent when borrowed from Germany.

Marquis of Salisbury (Robert Arthur Talbot Gascoyne Cecil), letter to Lord Lytton, viceroy of India, 27 April 1877

The future belongs to Russia, which grows and grows, looming above us as an increasingly terrifying nightmare.

Theobald von Bethmann Hollweg, German chancellor, 8 July 1914

Absolutism Tempered by Assassination

Ernst Friedrich Herbert Münster (1766–1839), Hanoverian diplomat, quoting 'an intelligent Russian' on the constitution of Russia under the Tsars.

In Russia, whatever be the appearance of things, violence and arbitrary rule is at the bottom of them all. Tyranny rendered calm by the influence of terror is the only kind of happiness which this government is able to afford its people.

Marquis de Custine, *Empire of the Czar: A Journey Through Eternal Russia* (1843)

Nothing is impossible in Russia but reform.

Michael, in Oscar Wilde's *Vera, or The Nihilists* (1880)

Back in the USSR

The Russian Revolution did not inspire all Western radicals:

If there's no dancing count me out.

Emma Goldman (1869–1940), Lithuanian-born US anarchist
and leftist

**From being a patriotic myth, the Russian people have
become an awful reality.**

Leon Trotsky, *The History of the Russian Revolution* (1931–3)

**There are no unemployed either in Russia or in
Dartmoor jail, and for the same reason.**

Philip Snowden, British Labour politician, 1932

**Gaiety is the most outstanding feature of the Soviet
Union.**

Joseph Stalin, in 1935, after watching collective-farm workers
putting on a display of folk dancing

Miles of cornfields, and ballet in the evening.

Alan Hackney, *Private Life* (1958), which was turned into the
film *I'm All Right, Jack* (1959)

**In the Soviet Union there is no mystical or obscure
treatment of love, such as decadent Western poets use.
We sing of how a young man falls in love with a girl
because of her industrial output.**

Stephan Petroviv

**Russian communism is the illegitimate child of Karl
Marx and Catherine the Great.**

Clement Attlee, speech at Aarhus University, 11 April 1956

In Russia they treated me like a Tsar – and you know how they treated the Tsar.
Bob Hope

Ronnie's Evil Empire

The Evil Empire.
President Ronald Reagan's characterization of the Soviet Union, borrowing from the Star Wars films. His original statement (8 March 1983) was: 'They are the focus of evil in the modern world.'

If the Soviet Union let another political party come into existence, they would still be a one-party state, because everybody would join the other party.
Remark to Polish Americans, 23 June 1983

My fellow Americans, I am pleased to tell you today that I've signed legislation which outlaws Russia for ever. The bombing begins in five minutes.
Radio test broadcast, 11 August 1984

Russian circus in town. Do not feed the animals.
Graffito, Czechoslovakia, 1968, during the Soviet invasion

In the United States you have freedom of speech. You can go up to Ronald Reagan and say, 'I don't like

Ronald Reagan.' In the Soviet Union you have the same thing. You can go up to Chernenko and say, 'I don't like Ronald Reagan.'

Yakov Smirnoff, Russian émigré comedian, quoted in *Newsweek*, 1984

Q: **What is a Russian string trio?**
A: **A Russian string quartet that has returned from the West.**

David Steel, quoted in the *Observer*, 1984

We pretend to work and they pretend to pay us.

Russian worker's joke, late 1980s

Marlboro Country: Glasnost and After

There is a discussion in my country about a new name for the USSR ... Philip Morris is sending us billions of cigarettes. So some people suggest our new name should be Marlboro Country.

Gennadi Gerasimov, in the *Sunday Times*, 29 October 1990

In the end we beat them with Levi 501 jeans. Seventy-two years of Communist indoctrination and propaganda was drowned out by a three-ounce Sony Walkman. A huge totalitarian system ... has been brought to its knees because nobody wants to wear Bulgarian shoes. ... Now they're lunch, and we're number one on the planet.

P.J. O'Rourke, 'The Death of Communism', in *Rolling Stone*, November 1989

Russia is an enormous lunatic asylum. There is a heavy padlock on the door, but there are no walls.
Tatyana Tolstaya, quoted in the *Guardian*, 19 March 1992

Nothing could discredit capitalism more than a decision of the Russians to try it.
Jack Tanner

The West continued to be worried about Russian nuclear weapons getting into the wrong hands. President George 'Dubya' Bush's secretary for defence, Donald Rumsfeld, called Russia

A nation of proliferators.

... while Rumsfeld's deputy, Paul Wolfowitz, diplomatically explained ...

These people will do anything for money.
Both quoted in the *Observer*, 25 March 2001

Horrorsville

Moscow ... is Horrorsville.
James Kirkup

Los Angeles without the sun or grass.
Lillian Hellman, referring to Moscow

Scandinavia: In the Realms of the Biking Kings

Don't talk to me about Norway, and Holland, and Sweden and all that rubbish. I'm talking about Royalty. Not bloody cloth-cap kings riding about on bikes. I mean, that's not Royalty. You'll never see our Queen on a bike. She wouldn't demean herself.

Johnny Speight, *The Thoughts of Chairman Alf (Alf Garnet's Little Blue Book)* (1973)

Uncouth Scandahoovians

There are a number of slang terms in the USA used for Scandinavian immigrants from *Norskis*, *Scowegians* and *Scandahoovians* to *Boxheads*, *Cottontops*, *Dumb socks* and *Herring chokers*.

An earlier view of the Scandinavians comes from a Holy Roman Emperor:

There are three fine old kingdoms, over which the King of Denmark is Lord, although their subjects are all rough and uncouth.

Emperor Maximilian I, letter to his daughter Margaret, 1 January 1516. At this time the kings of Denmark also ruled Norway and Sweden.

Denmark: Fun Capital of the World

From Hamlet to Kierkegaard, the word 'Danish' has been synonymous with fun, fun, fun ... Who else would have the sense of humor to stuff prunes and toecheese into lumps of wet dough and *serve it to you for breakfast?* ... Let's hear it for those very wonderful, kooky, very crazy, very whacky, very witty Danes! They're the *living end*! And vice versa.

Tony Hendra, 'EEC! It's the US of E!', in *National Lampoon*, 1976

Beer is the Danish national drink, and the Danish national weakness is another beer.

Clementine Paddleford (1898–1967)

To deprive a Dane of his boiled potatoes would be as cruel as depriving a baby of his bottle.

Nika Hazelton, *Danish Cooking* (1967)

Norway: The Sun Never Sets and the Bar Never Opens

I don't like Norwegians at all. The sun never sets, the bar never opens, and the whole country smells of kippers.

Evelyn Waugh, letter to Lady Diana Cooper, 13 July 1934

It is difficult to describe Norwegian charisma precisely but it is somewhere between a Presbyterian minister and a tree.

Johnny Carson, remark when Senator Walter Mondale was running against Ronald Reagan in the 1984 presidential elections. Mondale, of Norwegian ancestry, went by the nickname 'Norwegian Wood'.

The Norwegian language has been described as German spoken underwater.

Anonymous

Sweden: Their Heads are Too Square

'You disapprove of the Swedes?'
'Yes, sir.'
'Why?'
'Their heads are too square, sir.'

P.G. Wodehouse, *The Small Bachelor* (1927)

Racial characteristics: tedious, clean-living boy scout types, strangers to graffiti and littering but who are possessed of an odd suicidal mania. Speculation is that they're slowly boring themselves to death. This is certainly the case if their cars and movies are any indication.

P.J. O'Rourke, 'Foreigners Around the World', in *National Lampoon*, 1976

Like a Volvo, [Björn] Borg is rugged, has good after-sales service, and is very dull.

Clive James, in the *Observer*, 29 June 1980

Sweden is where they commit suicide and the king rides a bicycle.

Alan Bennett

First impression of Stockholm Paradise, second Limbo.

Evelyn Waugh, *Diary* (1947)

The Swedes are, despite their perceived boringness, noted for *Swedish culture*, i.e. rubber and PVC fetishism, and more tamely for just *Swedish*, i.e. mutual masturbation. Ironically, in the USA *Swedish headache* is intense sexual frustration.

Not So Bad as Iceland

Dublin, though a place much worse than London, is not so bad as Iceland.
Samuel Johnson, who visited neither Dublin nor Iceland

Reykjavik:
About as exciting as Aberdeen on a Saturday night.
Anonymous

Finland, A Nation of Drunken Captain Birds Eyes
A.A. Gill's description

Finland is the devil's country.
Russian saying

Switzerland: Bankers and Boredom

An Inferior Sort of Scotland

I look upon Switzerland as an inferior sort of Scotland.
Sydney Smith, letter to Lord Holland, 1815. And Smith didn't
think much of Scotland, as will be seen elsewhere ...

**Switzerland is simply a large, humpy, solid rock, with a
thin skin of grass stretched over it.**
Mark Twain, *A Tramp Abroad* (1880)

**Switzerland is a small, steep country, much more up
and down than sideways, and is all stuck over with
large brown hotels built in the cuckoo-clock style of
architecture.**
Ernest Hemingway, quoted in the *Toronto Star Weekly*,
4 March 1922

**The Swiss managed to build a lovely country around
their hotels.**
George Mikes, *Down with Everybody!* (1951)

**Switzerland only seems small because it's all folded
up. If you opened it out it would be bigger than the US.**
Neil Kinnock, quoted in *Time*, April 1997

She's like Switzerland – beautiful but dumb.
Anonymous

What a bloody country! Even the cheese has got holes in it.
Tom Stoppard, *Travesties* (1975)

They say that if the Swiss had designed these mountains [the Alps], they'd be rather flatter.
Paul Theroux, *The Great Railway Bazaar* (1975)

What Switzerland lacks is manure.
André Gide

The Little Gnomes of Zurich

The famous phrase referring to Swiss financiers was used by Harold Wilson in a speech in the House of Commons in 1964. It is thought to have been originated by George Brown in the sterling crisis of that year.

No more money, no more Swiss.
French saying, deriving from the time when Swiss mercenaries were the terror of Europe

The Swiss ... are not a people so much as a neat clean quite solvent business ...
William Faulkner, *Intruder in the Dust* (1948)

***Racial characteristics:* mountain Jews in whose icy clutches lay the fruits of grave misdeeds committed in every clime.**
P.J. O'Rourke, 'Foreigners Around the World', in *National Lampoon*, 1976

As the poet Dante once said, 'The hottest places in hell are reserved for those who, in a time of great moral crisis, maintain their neutrality.'
John F. Kennedy

The only nation I've ever been tempted to feel really racist about are the Swiss – a whole country of phobic handwashers living in a giant Barclay's Bank.
Jonathan Raban, *Arabia through the Looking Glass* (1979)

Switzerland has produced the numbered bank account, Ovaltine and Valium.
Peter Freedman

The Cuckoo-Clock Culture

The hatefulest thing in the world is a cuckoo clock.
Mark Twain, *Mark Twain's Notebook* (ed. A.B. Paine, 1935)

I don't like Switzerland; it has produced nothing but theologians and waiters.
Oscar Wilde, letter, 20 March 1899

In Italy for thirty years under the Borgias they had warfare, terror, murder, bloodshed – they produced Michelangelo, Leonardo da Vinci and the Renaissance. In Switzerland they had brotherly love, five hundred years of democracy and peace, and what did they produce? The cuckoo clock!
Orson Welles, lines contributed to Graham Greene's screenplay of the film *The Third Man* (1949)

You might as well run your head against a wall as talk to a Swiss.

French saying

Since its national products – snow and chocolate – both melt, the cuckoo clock was invented solely in order to give tourists something solid to remember it by.

Alan Coren, *The Sanity Inspector* (1974)

A country to be in for two hours, or two and a half if the weather is fine, and no more. Ennui comes in the third hour, and suicide attacks you before the night.

Lord Brougham (1778–1868)

The train passed through fruit farms and clean villages and Swiss cycling in kerchiefs, calendar scenes that you admire for a moment before feeling an urge to move on to a new month.

Paul Theroux, *The Great Railway Bazaar* (1975)

Faraway Countries
of Which We Know Nothing

How horrible, fantastic, incredible it is that we should be digging trenches and trying on gas masks here because of a quarrel in a faraway country between people of whom we know nothing.

Neville Chamberlain, radio broadcast, 27 September 1938, just before flying to Munich

Austria: Hopeless but Not Serious

The situation in Germany is serious but not hopeless; the situation in Austria is hopeless but not serious.

Austrian saying

A Bavarian is half-way between an Austrian and a human being.

Otto von Bismarck (1815–98)

The Austrian government ... is a system of despotism tempered by casualness.

Victor Adler, speech to the International Socialist Congress, Paris, 17 July 1889

Three Poles, Five Opinions

Where there are three Poles, there will be five opinions.

German saying

In the USA in the 19th century, Polish immigrants were known as *Flannel Mouths* or *Flannel Faces*; in the 20th century they became *Polacks*, which has continued to be an offensive term. A rather quaint 1940s' coinage for Poles was the rhyming slang *Sausage Rolls*.

In the 18th century Poland was dismembered by Prussia, Austria and Russia, and was not restored until the treaty of Versailles at the end of World War I. However, the Germans and the Russians still had their eyes on Poland:

That bastard of the Versailles treaty.
V.M. Molotov (1890–1986), Soviet statesman

I have no intention of maintaining a serious relationship with Poland.
Adolf Hitler, remark, 1934, when Germany terminated its non-aggression treaty with Poland

And contrast:
I desire the Poles carnally.
US president Jimmy Carter falls victim to a bad translation of 'I have come to listen to your opinions and hear your desires for the future', on a visit to Warsaw, 1978

Of course, the Germans and the Soviets carved up the country again in 1939. Polish resistance was gallant but hopeless:
We are not Poles. It could not happen here.
Maurice Gamelin, commander of French land forces, May 1940. It did happen there, and Gamelin was sacked later in the month as the Germans drove all before them.

The enmity of the Germans goes way back:
The Alps divide us from the Italians
From the French, the rivers separate us
The sea is between us and the English
But only hate keeps us and the Poles apart.
German rhyme, 18th century

The Pole has a large mouth, but nothing behind it.
German saying

The Russians are no friendlier:
A single Russian hair outweighs half a Pole.
Russian saying

Our eternal foes, the Poles.
Tsar Nicholas I, letter to his viceroy in Poland, Marshal
Paskievič, 7 May 1849

Some views from other parts of Europe:
Poland ... upon which has been lavished more false
sentiment, deluded sympathy, and amiable ignorance,
than on any subject of the present age.
Richard Cobden, pamphlet entitled *Russia* (1836)

There are few virtues that the Poles do not possess –
and there are few mistakes they have ever avoided.
Winston Churchill, speech, House of Commons, 16 August 1945

Poland has a ministry with four withouts: a minister of
education without schools, a cultus minister without
churches, a minister of justice without justice, and a
minister of the treasury without finances.
Polish saying

There are endless jokes about the supposed stupidity of Poles on the internet, mostly American in origin:

A Pole, a Brit and an American rob a bank. Afterwards, each hides in a different tree. The cops go to the American's tree and say, 'Who's up there?' The American guy says, 'Tweet, tweet.' The cops say, 'Oh, just a bird.' They go to the British guy's tree and say, 'Who's up there?' The British guy says, 'Meow, meow.' 'Oh, that's just the cat,' the cops say. So they go to the Polish guy's tree and say, 'Who's up there?' The Polish guy says, 'Moooooo!'

Boring Balts and Raging Magyars

Most Boring Tiny Enslaved Country: tiny enslaved Latvia.
National Lampoon, 1972, under the heading 'George Sanders says: "Here are some of the things that bored me to death."'

The Lithuanian is stupid like a pig but cunning like a serpent.
Polish saying

Coal and Cabbage

**Did you hear about the Polish airliner that crashed?
It ran out of coal.**

Q: **What is 200 yards long and eats cabbage?**
A: **A Polish meat queue.**

The new Polish navy has glass-bottom boats, to see the old Polish navy.

Where there is a Slav, there is a song; where a Magyar, there is a rage.
Slovak saying

Do not trust a Hungarian unless he has a third eye on his forehead.
Czech saying

Some Damned Silly Thing in the Balkans

If there is ever another war in Europe, it will come out of some damned silly thing in the Balkans.
Otto von Bismarck, remark to Ballen shortly before his death in 1898

God grant we may not have a European War thrust upon us, and for such a stupid reason too, no I don't mean stupid, but to have to go war on account of tiresome Serbia beggars belief.
Queen Mary, queen consort of George V, letter to her aunt, the grand duchess of Mecklenburg-Strelitz, 28 July 1914

The Yugoslav nation is a single people, with three religions and two alphabets.
Nicola Pašić (c.1846–1926), prime minister in the early 1920s. The saying is sometimes given as 'Yugoslavia is a country of six republics, five nationalities, four languages, three religions, two alphabets, but is still only one country.'

No wonder that Tito remarked in May 1980, shortly before his death:
I am the only Yugoslav.

The Americans don't really understand what's going on in Bosnia. To them it's the unspellables killing the unpronounceables.

P.J. O'Rourke, in the *Sun*, 1993

Even before all the violence, Yugoslavia wasn't too popular with some visitors:

It's a very long flight to Yugoslavia and you land in a field of full-grown corn. They figure it cushions the landing ... Now, at night, you can't do anything, because all of Belgrade is lit by a ten-watt light bulb, and you can't go anywhere, because Tito has the car. It was a beauty, a green '38 Dodge. And the food in Yugoslavia is either very good or very bad. One day, we arrived on location late and starving and they served us fried chains. When we got to our hotel rooms, mosquitoes as big as George Foreman were waiting for us. They were sitting in armchairs with their legs crossed.

Mel Brooks, interview in *Playboy*, 1975

Another fine place to drop in on is Albania ...

It's the sort of place you get into as late as possible, bring your own food, go to bed, get up, go for a walk, play the game and get out.

Jackie Charlton, English footballer

When a studio executive told Samuel Goldwyn that they could not make a film of Lillian Hellman's *The Children's Hour* because it dealt with lesbians:

OK, so we make them Albanians.

The British Isles

Inglan is a Bitch: Britain and England

Inglan is a bitch dere's no escapin' it
Inglan is a bitch dere's no runnin' way fram it.
Linton Kwesi Johnson, 'Inglan is a Bitch' (1980)

There is a good deal of muddle in the minds of foreigners and English people themselves as to the difference between 'English' and 'British', and between 'England' and 'Britain'. In contrast, the Irish, Welsh and above all the Scots are very clear as to who's who and what's what. As so many of the speakers below are extremely hazy as to the distinction, we make no effort beyond the feeblest to disentangle the mess, and leave interpretation to the reader's own prejudices.

Limeys, Poms and Rosbifs

Americans call Brits *Beefeaters*, *Hardheads* or *Limeys* (originally an Australian term, from the lime juice consumed on British naval vessels to ward off scurvy).

The Scottish term for the English, *Sassenachs*, is a Gaelic word, ultimately derived from 'Saxons'. *English Bastards* is now the more common term of abuse in Scotland. If they come to live in Scotland, they are known as *White Settlers*.

The French used to call the English *Les Rosbifs*, after the national dish, while to the Irish the English were *John Bull's Bastards*.

The Australians call Brits *Poms* or *Pommies*, and they are usually 'whingeing', as in:

Pass a law to give every single whingeing bloody Pommie his fare home to England. Back to the smoke and the sun shining ten days a year and shit in the streets. Yer can have it.

Thomas Keneally, *The Chant of Jimmie Blacksmith* (1972)

Apparently the word *Pom* comes from 'pomegranate', which supposedly sounds like 'immigrant' ... A rhyming-slang variant is *To-and-From*. Australians also call Brits *Lime-juicers* (see above) and *Kippers*, because they are 'two-faced with no guts'. Britain itself is *Fogland*, or *Pomgolia* to New Zealanders.

In South Africa, expat Brits are called *Rednecks* (because sunburnt) or *Soutpiels* – meaning 'salt-dicks', because they have one foot in England, one in South Africa, and the penis dangling in the salty ocean in between.

In American slang, *English*, as a noun, means deceptiveness and duplicity (from billiards jargon: an *English* is a spin put on the side of the ball). As an adjective, *English* means sado-masochistic (English men being famed abroad for their love of a good whipping), hence *English guidance*, bondage and discipline, and *English culture*, advertisements for such activities. In Europe, the *English disease* in the 18th century meant melancholy, then in the 19th century rickets, and from the 1960s a willingness to down tools and go on strike.

Sheep with a Nasty Side

Cyril Connolly's description of the British, or the English, quoted by Gavin Ewart in *Quarto*, 1980

Who the first inhabitants of Britain were, whether natives or immigrants, remains obscure; one must remember we are dealing with barbarians.

Tacitus, *Agricola* (AD 98)

Nemo bonus Brito est.
No good man is a Briton.

Ausonius, *Epigrams* 110

Wise men affirm it is the English way
Never to grumble till they come to pay.

Daniel Defoe, *Britannia*

She [England] is always diseased and suffering from differences, quarrels and hatred between her people.

Richard II, attributed remark in the Tower of London, 21 September 1399, shortly before his enforced abdication

That vain, ill-natured thing, an Englishman.

Daniel Defoe, *The True-Born Englishman* (1701)

England – a happy land we know,
Where follies naturally grow.

Charles Churchill, *The Ghost* (1763)

I should like my country well enough if it were not for my countrymen.

Horace Walpole, *Letters*

It must be acknowledged that the English are the most disagreeable of all the nations of Europe, more surly and morose, with less disposition to please, to exert

themselves for the good of society, to make small sacrifices, and to put themselves out of their way.

Sydney Smith

The English talk loudly and seem to care little for other people. This is their characteristic, and a very brutal and barbarous distinction it is.

Sydney Smith

For 'tis a low, newspaper, humdrum, lawsuit Country.

Lord Byron, *Don Juan* (1819–24), Canto xii, stanza 65

Rather Mad Norwegians

We do not regard Englishmen as foreigners. We look on them only as rather mad Norwegians.

Halvard Lange, Norwegian historian and politician, quoted in the *Observer*, 9 March 1957

I am sure my bones would not rest in an English grave, or my clay mix with the earth of that country. I believe the thought would drive me mad on my death-bed could I suppose that any of my friends would be base enough to convey my carcass back to her soil. I would not even feed her worms if I could help it.

Lord Byron, letter to John Murray, 7 June 1819. After he died in Greece, Byron's body was brought back to England and buried there.

A population sodden with drink, steeped in vice, eaten up by every social and physical malady, these are the denizens of Darkest England amidst whom my life has been spent.

William Booth, founder of the Salvation Army, *In Darkest England, and the Way Out* (1880)

A demon took a monkey to wife – the result, by the grace of God, was the English.

Indian saying

To disagree with three-fourths of the British public on all points is one of the first elements of sanity, one of the deepest consolations in all moments of spiritual doubt.

Oscar Wilde, lecture, 1882

A Disappointed Author

Curse the blasted, jelly-boned swines, the slimy, the belly-wriggling invertebrates, the miserable sodding rotters, the flaming sods, the snivelling, dribbling, palsied, pulseless lot that make up England. They've got white of egg in their veins, and their spunk is that watery it's a marvel they can breed ... Why, why, why, was I born an Englishman! – my cursed, rotten-boned, pappy-hearted countrymen, *why* was I sent to *them*?

D.H. Lawrence, letter to Edward Garnett, 3 July 1912, after a publisher had rejected *Sons and Lovers*

I am feeling a bit out of sympathy with England at present – God, what a hole, what witless crapulous people.
Philip Larkin, letter to Robert Conquest, 24 July 1955

Damn you, England. You're rotting now, and quite soon you'll disappear. My hate will outrun you yet if only for a few seconds. I wish it could be eternal.
John Osborne, letter to *Tribune*, August 1961

There are only three things against living in Britain: the place, the climate and the people.
Jimmy Edwards, comedian

We're no longer a nation of shopkeepers; we're a nation of cowboys.
Kirsty MacColl

England has become a squalid, uncomfortable, ugly place ... an intolerant, racist, homophobic, narrow-minded, authoritarian rat-hole run by vicious suburban-minded, materialistic philistines.
Hanif Kureishi, in 1988, quoted in Patrick Higgins (ed.), *A Queer Reader* (1993)

England's not a bad country ... It's just a mean, cold, ugly, divided, tired, clapped-out, post-imperial, post-industrial slag-heap covered in polystyrene hamburger cartons.
Margaret Drabble, *A Natural Curiosity* (1989)

England is a horrible place with horrible people, horrible food, horrible climate, horrible class system, horrible cities and horrible countryside.
Stephen Pile, in the *Sunday Times*

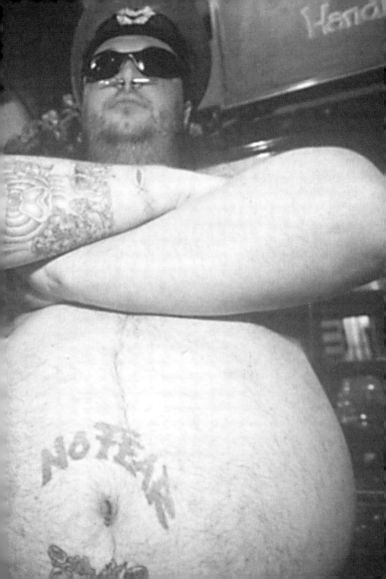

Isolated from the Whole World

And the Britons completely isolated from the whole world.
Virgil, *Eclogue* 1

England is set in the Ocean of Darkness. It is a considerable island, whose shape is that of the head of an ostrich ...
The 12th-century Arab scholar and geographer El-Edrisi.

Manchester

The shortest way out of Manchester is notoriously a bottle of Gordon's gin.
William Bolitho, *Twelve Against the Gods*, 'Caliogstro and Seraphina' (1930)

British Xenophobia takes the form of Insularism, and the Limeys all moved to an island some time ago to 'keep themselves to themselves', which as far as the rest of the world is concerned is a good thing.
The National Lampoon Encyclopedia of Humor (1973)

These are the heroes that despise the Dutch,
And rail at new-come foreigners so much;
Forgetting that themselves are all derived
From the most scoundrel race that ever lived.
A horrid medley of thieves and drones,
Who ransacked kingdoms, and dispeopled towns.
Daniel Defoe, *The True-Born Englishman* (1701)

He [the Briton] is a barbarian, and thinks that the customs of his tribe and island are the laws of nature.

George Bernard Shaw, *Caesar and Cleopatra* (pub. 1901)

They tell me that the English are a people who travel all over the world to laugh at other people.

Anonymous Spaniard, quoted in Gerald Brenan, *The Face of Spain* (1950)

It is, of course, a particularly British characteristic to think that every man is the same under the skin, and that Eskimos are really only would-be old Etonians wearing fur coats.

John Harvey-Jones, *Making It Happen* (1988)

Oxford

Oxford ... that old monkish place which I have a horror of.

Queen Victoria, remark, 31 October 1859

It's one thing being British
but you need a white skin to be English
then you can shout things in public places
at kids with a different complexion.

Tom Paulin, 'Chucking it Away' (after Heinrich Heine)

To be born an Englishman – ah, what an easy conceit that builds in you, what a self-righteous nationalism, a secure xenophobia, what a pride in your ignorance.

No other people speak so few languages. No other people ... have an expression that is the equivalent of 'greasy foreign muck'.

Tony Parsons, in *Arena* (BBC, 1989)

A Soggy Little Island: Views from America

A soggy little island huffing and puffing to keep up with Western Europe.

John Updike, 'London Life' (1969), in *Picked Up Pieces* (1976)

Racial characteristics: **cold-blooded queers with nasty complexions and terrible teeth who once conquered half the world but still haven't figured out central heating. They warm their beers and chill their baths and boil all their food.**

P.J. O'Rourke, 'Foreigners Around the World', in *National Lampoon*, 1976

A parasite spreading misery and ruin over the face of the Earth.

Thomas Jefferson

The self-complaisant British sneer.

Tom Taylor, *Abraham Lincoln*

If it is good to have one foot in England, it is still better, or at least as good, to have the other out of it

Henry James

Let us pause to consider the English,
Who when they pause to consider themselves they
**   get all reticently thrilled and tinglish,**

Because every Englishman is convinced of one thing, viz.: That to be an Englishman is to belong to the most exclusive club there is.

Ogden Nash, 'England Expects', in *I'm a Stranger Here Myself* (1938)

Living in England, provincial England, must be like being married to a stupid but exquisitely beautiful wife.

Margaret Halsey, *With Malice Toward Some* (1938)

All Englishmen talk as if they've got a bushel of plums stuck in their throats and then after swallowing them get constipated from the pits.

W.C. Fields

Q: **dwo**
we know of anything which can
be as dull as one englishman
A: **to**

e. e. cummings, *Complete Poems: 1910–1962* (1968)

The most dangerous thing in the world is to make a friend of an Englishman, because he'll come sleep in your closet rather than spend ten shillings on a hotel.

Truman Capote, remark, 1966

It is an interesting experience to become acquainted with a country through the eyes of the insane, and, if I may say so, a particularly useful grounding for life in Britain.

Bill Bryson, *Notes From a Small Island* (1995)

We are Colonized by Wankers: Scots on the English

Ah don't hate the English. They're just wankers. We are colonized by wankers. We can't even pick a decent, healthy culture to be colonized by.

Renton, in Irvine Welsh's *Trainspotting* (1993)

England Will Fight to the Last American

So joked US comedian Will Rogers. What some Brits regard as the 'Special Relationship' with the USA is something most Americans are unaware of – apart from the fact that they have more than once had to come to Britain's aid.

Oh, you English are so superior, aren't you? Well, would you like to know where you'd be without us, the old US of A, to protect you? I'll tell you. The smallest fucking province in the Russian Empire!

Kevin Kline as Otto in the film *A Fish Called Wanda* (1988), screenplay by John Cleese and Charles Crichton

The devellysche dysposicion of a Scottysh man, not to love nor favour an Englishe man.

Andrew Boorde, letter to Thomas Cromwell, 1536

England is not all the world.

Mary, Queen of Scots, remark at her trial, 1586

Bunchy knobs of papist flesh.

Scots pamphleteer on Charles I's bishops

The Englishman is never content but when he is grumbling.
Scottish saying

Minds like ours, my dear James, must always be above national prejudices, and in all companies it gives me true pleasure to declare, that, as a people, the English are very little inferior to the Scotch.
Christopher North, in *Blackwood's Edinburgh Magazine*, 1826

When asked the population of England, Thomas Carlyle said:
Thirty millions, mostly fools.

The world's busybody.
Thomas Carlyle, *Latter-Day Pamphlets* (1850)

A young Scotsman of your ability let loose upon the world with £300, what could he not do? It's almost appalling to think of; especially if he went among the English.
J.M. Barrie, *What Every Woman Knows* (1908)

The Most Pernicious Race of Vermin: Irish Views

I cannot but conclude the bulk of your natives to be the most pernicious race of little, odious vermin that Nature ever suffered to crawl upon the surface of the earth.
The king of Brobdingnag to Gulliver in Jonathan Swift's *Gulliver's Travels* (1726)

The Englishman has all the qualities of a poker except its occasional warmth.
Daniel O'Connell, 'the Liberator' (1775–1847)

... a typical Englishman, always dull and usually violent.
Oscar Wilde, *An Ideal Husband* (1895)

God is not an Englishman and truth will tell in time.
Dublin balladeer, 1916

If you eliminate smoking and gambling, you will be amazed to find that almost all an Englishman's pleasures can be, and mostly are, shared by his dog.
George Bernard Shaw

Englishmen hate two things – racial discrimination and Irishmen.
Anonymous Irishman

The leper of Europe.
Unnamed Irish minister, referring to Britain, quoted in the *Observer*, 11 March 2001, as the country plunged into the foot-and-mouth crisis

Perfidious Albion: The French on the Brits

L'Angleterre, ah, la perfide Angleterre ...
England, oh, perfidious England.
Jacques-Bénigne Bossuet (1627–1704), sermon on the circumcision, preached at Metz, 1652. The phrase was quoted by Napoleon as he left England for his final exile on St Helena.

At the time of the French Revolutionary wars the phrase became '*La perfide Albion*':
Let us attack in her own waters, perfidious Albion!
Augustin Ximénèz, 'L'Ère des Français' (October 1793)

From England, neither fair wind, nor good war.
French saying

By the time of the Hundred Years War, fear and loathing was well established:
England, the heart of a rabbit in the body of a lion, the jaws of a serpent in an abode of popinjays.
Eustache Deschamps (*c.* 1346–1406), French poet and civil servant

Deschamps described the English themselves as:
Poltroons, cowards, skulkers and dastards.

The perfidious, haughty, savage, disdainful, stupid, slothful, inhospitable, inhuman English.
Julius Caesar Scaliger (1484–1558), French classical scholar

Sot comme un Anglois.
Drunk as an Englishman.
François Rabelais, *Gargantua* (1534)

In all the four corners of the earth, one of these three names is given to him who steals from his neighbour – brigand, robber or Englishman.
Les Tirades de l'Anglais (1572)

They are naturally lazy, and spend half their time in taking tobacco.
Samuel Sorbière (1615–70), French translator of Thomas Hobbes

The English have always been a wicked race.
Charlotte Elizabeth, duchess of Orléans, letter to her stepsister Louisa, 13 January 1718

The English, who eat their meat red and bloody, show the savagery that goes with such food.

Julien Offray de La Mettrie (1709–51), French physician and philosopher

Boney's Beefs

The English have no exalted sentiments. They can all be bought.

Napoleon I

England is a nation of shopkeepers.

Napoleon I

I tell you Wellington is a bad general and the English are bad soldiers. I will settle this matter by lunch time.

Napoleon briefs his commanders before Waterloo

The whole world needs France when England needs the whole world.

Antoine de Rivarol, *Discours sur l'universalité de la langue française* (1784)

Don't trust any Englishman who speaks French with a correct accent.

French saying

The English are, I think, the most obscure and barbarous people in the world.

Stendhal (1783–1842)

A nation of ants, morose, frigid, and still preserving the same dread of happiness and joy as in the days of John Knox.

Max O'Rell (Paul Blouet), *John Bull et son Île* (1883)

Do not forget that the Englishman's soul is like the English skies: the weather is nearly always bad, but the climate is good.

André Maurois, *Three Letters on the English* (1938)

To make a union with Great Britain would be fusion with a corpse.

Henri Philippe Pétain, referring to Churchill's proposal of a political union with France in 1940, quoted in Winston Churchill, *Their Finest Hour* (1949)

I cannot believe that the great British people, in order to protect their identity, would now be cowering on the very island from which they set sail to travel the world.

Édouard Balladur, French prime minister, referring to British Euroscepticism, May 1994

We are all too inclined to see [England] as a production line for tattooed, alcoholic and dangerous hooligans.

Le Monde, July 1998, during the World Cup competition held in France

You never hear debates about ethics or morals here, just about saving money. It's no wonder the place is falling apart. Britain really is a nation of shopkeepers.
Patrice Claude, London correspondent of *Le Monde*, 10 March 2001

Go away. This evil has come to us from your whore of an England, once again.
Anonymous French farmer speaking during the foot-and-mouth crisis of 2001

Unmitigated Noodles: The Germans on the Brits

It was Kaiser Wilhelm II who called the British 'unmitigated noodles'. He should have known: his grandmother was Queen Victoria.

On another occasion the Kaiser blustered:
It is my royal and imperial command ... that you address all your skill, and all the valour of my soldiers, to exterminate the treacherous English, and to walk over General French's contemptible little army.
Kaiser Wilhelm II, Army Order, Aix, 19 August 1914. Actually, the German word used by Wilhelm more closely approximates 'negligible'. Either via an error of translation, or through propagandist machinations, the Army Order became the origin of the name that the first British Expeditionary Force proudly bore at the outset of World War I – the 'Old Contemptibles'.

French and Russian they matter not,
A blow for a blow and a shot for a shot! ...
We have one foe and one alone, England!

Ernst Lissauer, 'Hassgesang Gegen England' (1914)

Asked what he would do if the British army landed on the coast
of Germany:
I would call out the police to arrest them.

Otto von Bismarck

- -

Slough

**Come, friendly bombs, and fall on Slough.
It isn't fit for humans now.**

John Betjeman, 'Slough' (1937)

- -

**It is related of an Englishman that he hung himself to
avoid the daily task of dressing and undressing.**

Johann Wolfgang von Goethe

**From every Englishman emanates a kind of gas, the
deadly choke-damp of boredom.**

Heinrich Heine

The English are the people of consummate cant.

Friedrich Nietzsche, *Twilight of the Idols* (1889)

The English think soap is civilization.

Heinrich von Treitschke (1834–96), German historian and
advocate of power politics

According to the English there are two countries in the world today which are led by adventurers: Germany and Italy. But England, too, was led by adventurers when she built her Empire. Today she is ruled by incompetents.

Adolf Hitler, remark to Count Ciano, Mussolini's foreign minister

The British, as usual, will fight to the last Frenchman.

German propaganda, *c.* 1940

Paralytic sycophants.
Effete betrayers of humanity.
Carrion-eating servile imitators.
Arch-cowards and collaborators.
Gang of women-murderers.
Degenerate rabble.
Parasitic traditionalists.
Playboy soldiers.
Conceited dandies.

Officially sanctioned terms for the British in Communist East Germany, *c.* 1951

Why do you look like freshly cooked lobsters after one day on the beach?

The German tabloid newspaper *Bildzeitung* responds to xenophobic German-bashing headlines in English tabloid newspapers prior to England's semi-final match with Germany in the European championship finals, June 1996.

A Family with the Wrong Members in Control

England ... resembles a family, a rather stuffy Victorian family, with not many black sheep in it but with all its cupboards bursting with skeletons. It has rich relations who have to be kow-towed to and poor relations who are horribly sat upon, and there is a deep conspiracy about the source of the family income. It is a family in which the young are generally thwarted and most of the power is in the hands of irresponsible uncles and bedridden aunts. Still, it is a family ... with the wrong members in control.

George Orwell, 'England, Your England' (1941)

We are a nation of governesses.

George Bernard Shaw, in the *New Statesman*, 12 April 1913

England is ... a country infested with people who love to tell us what to do, but who very rarely seem to know what's going on.

Colin MacInnes, *England, Half English*, 'Pop Songs and Teenagers' (1961)

The government of the world I live in was not framed, like that of Britain, in after-dinner conversations over the wine.

Henry David Thoreau, *Walden* (1854)

Englishmen never will be slaves: they are free to do whatever the Government and public opinion allow them to do.

The Devil in George Bernard Shaw's *Man and Superman* (1903)

Freedom of speech in England is little else than the right to write or say anything which a jury of twelve shopkeepers think it expedient should be said or written.
Albert Venn Dicey, introduction to *Study of the Law of the Constitution* (1885)

Freedom of the press in Britain is freedom to print such of the proprietor's prejudices as the advertisers don't object to.
Hannen Swaffer (1879–1962), English journalist, *c.* 1928, quoted in Tom Driberg, *Swaff* (1974)

Political toleration is a by-product of the complacency of the ruling class. When that complacency is disturbed there never was a more bloody-minded set of thugs than the British ruling class.
Michael Foot

God Wouldn't Trust an Englishman in the Dark

I know why the sun never sets on the British Empire; God wouldn't trust an Englishman in the dark.
Duncan Spaeth

England ... watches like a wolf a chance for plunder ...
Ralph Waldo Emerson, *Journals*

A small boy with diamonds is no match for a large burglar with experience.
Anonymous, referring to the British war against the Boers, in *Life*, 15 November 1900

What about Wednesday Week?

If I wrote a book about England I should call it 'What about Wednesday Week?' which is what English people say when they are making what they believe to be an urgent appointment.

Claud Cockburn, *In Time of Trouble* (1956)

Would it be possible to stand still on one spot more majestically – while simulating a triumphant march forward – than it is done by the two English Houses of Parliament?

Alexander Herzen (1812–70), Russian writer, *My Past and Thoughts* (pub. 1921)

In England we have come to rely upon a comfortable time-lag of fifty years or a century intervening between the perception that something ought to be done and a serious attempt to do it.

H.G. Wells, *The Work, Wealth and Happiness of Mankind* (1931)

No more distressing moment can ever face a British government than that which requires it to come to a hard, fast and specific decision.

Barbara Tuchman, *The Guns of August* (1962), referring to August 1914

We have a system of government with the engine of a lawnmower and the brakes of a Rolls-Royce.

Jonathan Lynn and Antony Jay, *Yes, Prime Minister*, 'A Real Partnership' (1987)

'What shall it profit a man if he shall gain the whole world and lose his own soul?' That must be why England gained the whole world.

Oliver St John Gogarty, *Going Native* (1940)

We seem, as it were, to have conquered and peopled half the world in a fit of absence of mind.

J.R. Seeley (1834–95), lecture entitled 'The Expansion of England'

The English are mentioned in the Bible: Blessed are the meek, for they shall inherit the earth.

Mark Twain, *Following the Equator* (1897)

The English send all their bores abroad, and acquired the Empire as a punishment.

Edward Bond, *The Narrow Road to the Deep North* (1968)

Englishmen are distinguished by their traditions and
  ceremonials,
And also by their affection for their colonies and their
  condescension to their colonials.

Ogden Nash, 'England Expects', in *I'm a Stranger Here Myself* (1938)

Now that we don't have a war, what's wrong with a good punch-up? We are a nation of yobs. Without that characteristic, how did we colonize the world? I don't agree with broken glass and knives. But what an English guy does is fight with his fists; a good clean fight. With so many milksops, left-wing liberals and

wetties around, I just rejoice that there are people who keep up our historic spirit.

The Dowager Marchioness of Reading, on the violence perpetrated by English fans during the 1998 World Cup Finals in France

The Dirty Armpit of Europe: Britain's Decline

We are the dirty armpit of Europe.

Ken Livingstone, quoted in the *Independent*, 18 March 1989

We have been Europe's sink, the jakes where she Voids all her offal out-cast progeny.

Daniel Defoe, *The True-Born Englishman* (1701) ('jakes' = lavatory)

The people of England are never so happy as when you tell them they are ruined.

Arthur Murray, *The Upholsterers* (1758)

Northerners

People in the North die of ignorance and crisps.
Edwina Currie, as junior health minister,
September 1986

Northerners are far too busy breeding pigeons, eating deep-fried chip butties and executing drive-by shootings on Moss Side to dally over the new Sebastian Faulks.
Hildy Johnson, in the *Bookseller*, 9 March 2001

Britain today is suffering from galloping obsolescence.
Tony Benn, speech, 31 January 1963

Britain has lost its pride but retained its conceit.
Reginald Maudling

The country is going down the drain and they are squabbling about the size of the plughole.
Jeremy Thorpe

Present policies are leading us to the status of a banana republic that has run out of bananas.
Richard Marsh, quoted in the *Daily Telegraph*, 6 September 1978

Of Britain under Margaret Thatcher:
A cross between Singapore and Telford.
Peter Cook, in the *Guardian*, 23 July 1988

Britain's 'present stature':
Italy with rockets.
Andrew Roberts, Introduction to *Eminent Churchillians* (1994)

Failure is All the Rage

In England, failure is all the rage.
Quentin Crisp, *The Naked Civil Servant* (1968)

The English public always feels perfectly at its ease when a mediocrity is talking to it.
Oscar Wilde, 'The Critic As Artist' (1890)

It is beginning to be hinted that we are a nation of amateurs.
Lord Rosebery (Archibald Philip Primrose), rectorial address, Glasgow University, 16 November 1900

The English instinctively admire any man who has no talent and is modest about it.

James Agate, *Ego 9* (1948)

The English never draw a line without blurring it.

Winston Churchill, speech, House of Commons, 16 November 1948

You only have to survive in England and all is forgiven you ... if you can eat a boiled egg at ninety in England they think you deserve a Nobel Prize.

Alan Bennett, remark on *The South Bank Show* (LWT, 1984). He reused the line in *An Englishman Abroad* (1989).

The English think incompetence is the same thing as sincerity.

Quentin Crisp, quoted in the *New York Times*, 1977

There is such relish in England for anything that doesn't succeed.

Jonathan Miller, interview in the *Sunday Times*, 4 December 1988

There's nothing the British like better than a bloke who comes from nowhere, makes it, and then gets clobbered.

Melvyn Bragg, quoted in the *Guardian*, 23 September 1988

Here is a country that won a noble war, dismantled a mighty empire in a generally benign and enlightened way, created a far-seeing welfare state – in short, did nearly everything right – and then spent the rest of the century looking on itself as a dismal failure.

Bill Bryson, *Notes From a Small Island* (1995)

The Most Embarrassed People in the World

They are the most embarrassed people in the world, the English.

Alan Bennett, *The Old Country* (1977)

A Quadrille in a Sentry-Box: English Conversation

Most English talk is a quadrille in a sentry-box.

The Duchess, in Henry James's *The Awkward Age* (1889)

When two Englishmen meet their first talk is of the weather.

Samuel Johnson, in *The Idler*, 24 June 1758

Silence – a conversation with an Englishman.

Heinrich Heine

An Englishman's never so natural as when he's holding his tongue.

Isabel Archer, in Henry James's *The Portrait of a Lady* (1881)

Do you have any idea what it's like being English, being so correct all the time, being so stifled by this dread of doing the wrong thing? We are all terrified of embarrassment ... That's why we're so ... dead.

John Cleese, as the repressed lawyer Archie Leach in the film *A Fish Called Wanda* (1988), screenplay by Cleese and Charles Crichton

It is not that the Englishman can't feel – it is that he is afraid to feel. He has been taught at his public school that feeling is bad form. He must not express great joy or sorrow, or even open his mouth too wide when he talks – his pipe might fall out if he did.

E.M. Forster, 'Notes on the English Character' (1920)

Not only England, but every Englishman is an island.

Novalis (1772–1801), German Romantic writer and poet, in 1799

Even crushed against his brother in the Tube the average Englishman pretends desperately that he is alone.

Germaine Greer, *The Female Eunuch* (1970)

I've always said, if you want to outwit an Englishman, touch him when he doesn't want to be touched.

Julian Barnes, *Talking It Over* (1991)

The English are very good at hiding emotions, but without suggesting there is anything passionate to hide.

David Hare, in the *Observer* Magazine, 26 May 1989

In England there is only silence or scandal.

André Maurois (1885–1967)

The English take their pleasures sadly after the fashion of their country.

Duc de Sully (1559–1641), *Memoirs*

The Pleasures of Ill Health

The English find ill-health not only interesting but respectable and often experience death in an effort to avoid a fuss.

Pamela Frankau, *Pen to Paper* (1961)

The sneeze in English is the harbinger of misery, even death. I sometimes think the only pleasure an Englishman has is in passing on his cold germs.

Gerald Durrell, *My Family and Other Animals* (1956)

A Stony British Stare: The Snotty English

And curving a contumelious lip,
Gorgonized me from head to foot,
With a stony British stare.

Alfred, Lord Tennyson, *Maud* (1855)

'It is in bad taste,' is the most formidable word an Englishman can pronounce.

Ralph Waldo Emerson, *Journals*, 1839

Toward people with whom they disagree, the English gentry, or at any rate that small cross-section of them I have seen, are tranquilly good-natured. It is not *comme il faut* to establish the supremacy of an idea by smashing in the faces of all the people who try to contradict it. The English never smash it in the face. They merely refrain from asking it to dinner.

Margaret Halsey, *With Malice Toward Some* (1938)

The Englishman, be it noted, seldom resorts to violence; when he is sufficiently goaded he simply opens up, like the oyster, and devours his adversary.

Henry Miller, *The Wisdom of the Heart*, 'Raimu' (1941)

The English don't raise their voices, Arthur, although they may have other vulgarities.

Lillian Hellman, *Pentimento*, 'Arthur W.A. Cowan' (1973)

Brains! I Don't Believe in Brains

Brains! I don't believe in brains. You haven't any, I know, sir.

The Duke of Cambridge, commander-in-chief of the British army, 1854–95

Of all nations in the world the English are perhaps least a nation of pure philosophers.

Walter Bagehot, *The English Constitution* (1867)

One has often wondered whether upon the whole earth there is anything so unintelligent, so unapt to perceive how the world is really going, as an ordinary young Englishman of our upper class.

Matthew Arnold, *Culture and Anarchy* (1869)

Thinking is the most unhealthy thing in the world, and people die of it just as they die of any other disease. Fortunately, in England at any rate, thought is not catching.

Oscar Wilde, *The Decay of Lying* (1889)

Ignorance is like a delicate exotic fruit; touch it and the bloom is gone. The whole theory of modern education is radically unsound. Fortunately, in England, at any rate, education produces no effect whatsoever. If it did, it would prove a serious danger to the upper classes, and probably lead to acts of violence in Grosvenor Square.

Lady Bracknell, in Oscar Wilde's *The Importance of Being Earnest* (1895)

The English are not an inventive people; they don't eat enough pie.

Thomas Alva Edison (1847–1931)

No Englishman has any common sense, or ever had, or ever will have.

George Bernard Shaw, *John Bull's Other Island* (1904)

The intelligent are to the intelligentsia what a gentleman is to a gent.

Stanley Baldwin, prime minister, quoted in G.M. Young, *Stanley Baldwin* (1952)

The English think of an opinion as something which a decent person, if he has the misfortune to have one, does all he can to hide.

Margaret Halsey, *With Malice Toward Some* (1938)

To the man-in-the-street who, I'm sorry to say,
Is a keen observer of life,
The word Intellectual suggests straight away
A man who's untrue to his wife.

W.H. Auden, 'Notes on Intellectuals' (1947)

Of the general inadequacy of intellect in the conduct of life Britain is the most majestic exponent.

Freya Stark, *Perseus in the Wind* (1948)

Always in England if you had the type of brain that was capable of understanding T.S. Eliot's poetry or Kant's logic, you could be sure of finding large numbers of people who would hate you violently.

D.J. Taylor, in the *Guardian*, 14 September 1989

Only in Britain could it be thought a defect to be 'too clever by half'. The probability is that too many people are too stupid by three-quarters.

John Major, quoted in the *Observer*, 7 July 1991

A Land of Snobbery and Privilege

England is the most class-ridden country under the sun. It is a land of snobbery and privilege, ruled largely by the old and silly.

George Orwell, *The Lion and the Unicorn* (1941)

An Englishman loves a lord.

English saying

Whenever he met a great man he grovelled before him, and my-lorded him as only a free-born Briton can do.

William Makepeace Thackeray, *Vanity Fair* (1847–8)

Better a brutal starving nation,
Than men with thoughts above their station.

John Masefield, *The Everlasting Mercy* (1911)

London – the Great Wen

But what is to be the fate of the great wen of all? The monster, called ... 'the metropolis of the empire'?
William Cobbett, *Rural Rides* (1822)

I would sell London, if I could find a suitable purchaser.
Richard I, *c.* 1189, attempting to raise money for the Third Crusade, quoted in William of Newburgh, *Historia Rerum Anglicarum* (1196–8)

The truth is, that in London it is always a sickly season. Nobody is healthy in London, nobody can be.
Mr Woodhouse, in Jane Austen's *Emma* (1816)

That monstrous tuberosity of civilized life, the capital of England.
Teufelsdröckh, in Thomas Carlyle's *Sartor Resartus* (1833–4)

London is a large village on the Thames where the

Of the British officer:
He muffs his real job without a blush, and yet he would rather be shot than do his bootlaces up criss-cross.
H.G. Wells, *Mr Britling Sees It Through* (1916)

In England when a new character appears in our circles the first question always is, 'Who is he?' In France it is, 'What is he?' In England, 'How much a year?' In France, 'What has he done?'
Benjamin Disraeli, *Coningsby* (1844)

principal industries carried on are music halls and the confidence trick.
Dan Leno (1860–1904), music-hall entertainer

London, that great cesspool into which all the loungers of the Empire are irresistibly drained.
Arthur Conan Doyle, *A Study in Scarlet* (1887)

London is too full of fogs – and serious people. Whether the fogs produce the serious people or whether the serious people produce the fogs, I don't know, but the whole thing rather gets on my nerves.
Oscar Wilde, *Lady Windermere's Fan* (1892)

When it's three o'clock in New York, it's still 1938 in London.
Bette Midler, quoted in *The Times*, 21 September 1978.
Something similar has been attributed to Groucho Marx.

I can trace my ancestry back to a protoplasmal primordial atomic globule. Consequently, my family pride is something inconceivable. I can't help it. I was born sneering.
Pooh-Bah, in W.S. Gilbert's *The Mikado* (1885)

In England, Justice is open to all, like the Ritz hotel.
Sir James Mathew (1830–1908), Irish judge, quoted by R.E. Megarry in *Miscellany-at-Law* (1955)

The Peerage is one book a young man about town should know thoroughly and it is the best thing in fiction the English have ever done.

Oscar Wilde, *A Woman of No Importance* (1893)

How superbly brave is the Englishman in the presence of the awfulest forms of danger & death; & how abject in the presence of any & all forms of hereditary rank.

Mark Twain, *Mark Twain's Notebooks and Journals* (ed. Frederick Anderson, 1979)

You never find an Englishman among the underdogs – except in England, of course.

Evelyn Waugh, *The Loved One* (1948)

A broad definition of crime in England is that it is any lower-class activity that is displeasing to the upper class.

David Frost and Antony Jay, *To England with Love* (1967)

Britain is a society where the ruling class does not rule, the working class does not work, and the middle class is not in the middle.

George Mikes, *English Humour for Beginners* (1980)

Chelmsford

If any one were to ask me what in my opinion was the dullest and most stupid spot on the face of the Earth, I should decidedly say Chelmsford.

Charles Dickens, letter, 1835

The two sides of industry have traditionally loathed each other in Britain with the greatest possible loathing, mistrust and contempt. They are both absolutely right.

Auberon Waugh, in *Private Eye*, 1983

Too Much Couth: English Manners

English life, while very pleasant, is rather bland. I expected kindness and gentility and I found it, but there is such a thing as too much couth.

S.J. Perelman, quoted in the *Observer*, 24 September 1971

An Englishman, even if he is alone, forms an orderly queue of one.

George Mikes, *How to be an Alien* (1946)

In England it is bad manners to be clever, to assert something confidently. It may be your personal view that two and two make four, but you must not state it in a self-assured way, because this is a democratic country and others may be of a different opinion.

George Mikes, *How to be an Alien* (1946)

The English are polite by telling lies.

Malcolm Bradbury, *Stepping Westward* (1965)

If an Englishman gets run down by a truck, he apologises to the truck.

Jackie Mason, American comedian, quoted in the *Independent*, 20 September 1990

'Twas not always so ...

The English (it must be owned) are rather a foul-mouthed nation.
William Hazlitt, 'On Criticism' (1821–2)

Englishmen are not made of polishable substance.
Nathaniel Hawthorne, *Journals*, 13 February 1854

Belching at table, and in all companies whatsoever, is a thing which the English no more scruple than they do coughing and sneezing.
H. Misson de Valbourg (1656–1723)

If it weren't for his good manners, Leopold could easily pass for an Englishman.
Norman Ginsbury, *The First Gentleman* (1946)

The Most Rigid Code of Immorality

I like the English. They have the most rigid code of immorality in the world.
Malcolm Bradbury, *Eating People is Wrong* (1959)

You must look out in Britain that you are not cheated by the charioteers.
Cicero

Like an English oath.
Dutch simile, meaning 'worthless'

The English are, in my opinion, perfidious and cunning, plotting the destruction of the lives of foreigners, so

that even if they humbly bend the knee, they cannot be trusted.

Leo de Rozmital (1468–1510)

We know no spectacle so ridiculous as the British public in one of its periodical fits of morality.

Thomas Babington Macaulay, 'Moore's *Life of Lord Byron*', in *Essays Contributed to the Edinburgh Review* (1843)

As thorough an Englishman as ever coveted his neighbour's goods.

Charles Kingsley, *The Water-Babies* (1862–3)

There is nothing so bad or so good that you will not find an Englishman doing it; but you will never find an Englishman in the wrong. He does everything on principle. He fights you on patriotic principles; he robs you on business principles; he enslaves you on imperial principles; he bullies you on manly principles; he supports his king on loyal principles and cuts off his king's head on republican principles. His watchword is always Duty; and he never forgets that the nation which lets its duty get on the opposite side to its interest is lost.

Napoleon, in George Bernard Shaw's *The Man of Destiny* (1898)

Your pious English habit of regarding the world as a moral gymnasium built expressly to strengthen your character in.

George Bernard Shaw, *Man and Superman* (1903)

An Englishman thinks he is moral when he is only uncomfortable.

The Devil, in George Bernard Shaw's *Man and Superman* (1903)

The Englishman never enjoys himself except for a noble purpose.

A.P. Herbert, *Uncommon Law* (1935)

The Anglo-Saxon conscience does not prevent the Anglo-Saxon from sinning; it merely prevents him from enjoying his sin.

Salvador de Madariaga (1886–1978), Spanish historian and diplomat

The thing about the British conscience, you see, is that it really has no more capacity than … a primitive home computer, if you like. It can hold two or three things in its memory at a time.

Jonathan Coe, *What a Carve Up!* (1994)

The British do not expect happiness. I had the impression, all the time that I lived there, that they do not want to be happy; they want to be right.

Quentin Crisp, 'Love Lies Bleeding' (1991)

To be associated with the British is to be offered the choice of one of two bags tied at the neck with string. One contains a viper, the other a bag of gold. If you are lucky, you will choose the bag of gold, only to find that the British have

reserved the right to exchange it for the other without notice. Conversely, ill luck might cause you to pick the bag with the viper, whereupon the British will wait until you have been bitten, and then say, 'We didn't mean it; have this other bag.'

Louis de Bernières, *Captain Corelli's Mandolin* (1994)

No Sex Please, We're British

Title of a 1960s' farce by Anthony Marriott and Alistair Foot

Continental people have a sex life; the English have hot-water bottles.

George Mikes, *How to be an Alien* (1946)

The cold of the polar regions was nothing to the chill of an English bedroom.

Fridtjof Nansen (1861–1930), Norwegian explorer, quoted in Daniele Vare, *The Laughing Diplomat* (1939)

I did a picture in England one winter and it was so cold I almost got married.

Shelley Winters, quoted in the *New York Times*, 29 April 1956

One of my ministers found half-naked with a guardsman in Hyde Park? Last Wednesday? The coldest night of the year? Makes you proud to be British.

Winston Churchill, allegedly

It has to be admitted that we English have sex on the brain, which is a very unsatisfactory place to have it.

Malcolm Muggeridge, 'Ideas and Men', in the *New York Times*, 11 October 1964

Cricket-playing nations are capable of only limited amounts of sexual activity.
Letter published in the *Bangkok Post*, 1991

English culture is basically homosexual in the sense that the men only really care about other men.
Germaine Greer, in the *Daily Mail*, 18 April 1988

In Anglo-Saxon countries men prefer the company of other men. ... In England 25 per cent of men are homosexual.
Edith Cresson, French prime minister, in 1991

I couldn't believe it the other day when I picked up a British newspaper and read that 82 per cent of men would rather sleep with a goat than me.
The Duchess of York, quoted in the *Observer*, 25 March 2001

Most Englishmen can never get over the embarrassing fact that they were born in bed with a woman.
Anonymous Scotsman

Our Chilly Women

Our cloudy climate and our chilly women.
Lord Byron, *Beppo* (1818), stanza 49

**This Englishwoman is so refined
She has no bosom and no behind.**
Stevie Smith, 'The Englishwoman' (1937)

Contrary to popular belief, English women do not wear tweed nightgowns.
Hermione Gingold, in the *Saturday Review*, 1955

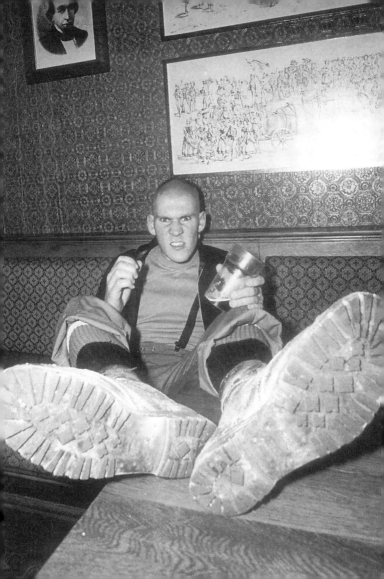

They say a woman should be a cook in the kitchen and a whore in bed. Unfortunately, my wife is a whore in the kitchen and a cook in bed.

Anonymous man from Sunderland, quoted in Geoffrey Gorer, *Exploring English Character* (1955)

Englishwomen's shoes look as if they had been made by someone who had often heard shoes described, but had never seen any.

Margaret Halsey, *With Malice Toward Some* (1938)

England is the paradise of women, the purgatory of men, and the hell of horses.

John Florio, *Second Fruits* (1591)

In England I would rather be a man, a horse, a dog or a woman, in that order. In America I think the order would be reversed.

Bruce Gould

Boy George is all England needs – another queen who can't dress.

Joan Rivers

Summer Has Set In with Its Usual Severity

Samuel Taylor Coleridge, letter to Vincent Novello, 9 May 1826

The way to ensure summer in England is to have it framed and glazed in a comfortable room.

Horace Walpole, letter to William Cole, 28 May 1774

The English winter – ending in July,
To recommence in August ...
Lord Byron, *Don Juan* (1819–24), Canto xiii, stanza 42

We are all well, and keep large fires, as it behoveth
those who pass their summers in England.
Sydney Smith, letter to Mrs Meynell, 1820

An English summer, two fine days and a thunderstorm.
M.A. Denham, *A Collection of Proverbs ... Relating to the*
Weather (1846)

'Tis the hard grey weather
Breeds hard English men.
Charles Kingsley, 'Ode to the North-East Wind' (1854)

In this country there are only two seasons, winter and
winter.
Shelagh Delaney, *A Taste of Honey* (1958)

If God had intended man to live in England, he'd have
given him gills.
David Renwick and Andrew Marshall, *The Burkiss Way* (BBC
Radio, 11 November 1980)

The climate of England has been the world's most
powerful colonizing influence.
Russell Green

Rain is the one thing the British do better than
anybody else.
Marilyn French

The British, he thought, must be gluttons for satire: even the weather forecast seemed to be some kind of spoof, predicting every possible combination of weather for the next twenty-four hours without actually committing itself to anything specific.

David Lodge, *Changing Places* (1975)

I have a small, tattered clipping that I sometimes carry with me and pull out for purposes of private amusement. It's a weather forecast from the *Western Daily Mail* and it says, in toto: 'Outlook: Dry and warm, but cooler with some rain.'

Bill Bryson, *Notes From a Small Island* (1995)

The Graces Do Not Seem to be Natives of Great Britain

It must be owned, that the Graces do not seem to be natives of Great Britain; and I doubt, the best of us here have more of rough than polished diamond.

Lord Chesterfield, *Letters to His Son* (1774), 18 November 1748

So little, England. Little music. Little art. Timid. Tasteful. Nice.

Alan Bennett, *An Englishman Abroad* (1983)

England has civilization but no culture.

Robin Mathews

Philistinism! – We have not the word in English. Perhaps we have not the word because we have so much of the thing.

Matthew Arnold, *Essays in Criticism*, First Series (1865)

In England it is enough for a man to try and produce any serious, beautiful work to lose all his rights as a citizen.
Oscar Wilde, lecture, 1882

The English public, as a mass, takes no interest in a work of art until it is told that the work in question is immoral.
Oscar Wilde, letter to the *St James's Gazette*, 27 June 1890, regarding the reception of his novel *The Picture of Dorian Gray*

More Heritage Than is Good for Them

It sometimes occurs to me that the British have more heritage than is good for them.
Bill Bryson, *Notes From a Small Island* (1995)

Had Jerusalem been built in England and the site of the Crucifixion discovered, it would promptly be built over and called the Golgotha Centre.
Alan Bennett

The attitude of the English toward English history reminds one a good deal of the attitude of a Hollywood director toward love.
Margaret Halsey, *With Malice Toward Some* (1938)

It will be said of this generation that it found England a land of beauty and left it a land of beauty spots.
C.E.M. Joad, quoted in the *Observer*, 31 May 1953

The English have a miraculous power of turning wine into water.

Oscar Wilde

The British public has always had an unerring taste for ungifted amateurs.

John Osborne, 1957

Definition of the British genius:

An infinite capacity for making drains.

Dr Lilian Knowles, quoted in Kingsley Martin, *Father Figures* (1966)

Nothing on Earth More Terrible: British Art

There is nothing on earth more terrible than English music, except English painting.

Heinrich Heine, *Lutezia* (1854)

I think it owing to the good sense of the English that they have not painted better.

William Hogarth, letter to Horace Walpole, 1761

What you call English Art, is not Art at all, but produce, of which there is, and always has been, and always will be, a plenty.

James McNeill Whistler, *The Gentle Art of Making Enemies* (1890)

An Englishman doesn't trust his intuition. An Englishman will say, 'I like that picture but I don't know whether I *ought* to like it. What shall I do? I'll have to wait and see what the general feeling is.'

L.S. Lowry, quoted in Allen Andrews, *The Life of L.S. Lowry* (1977)

British sculpture:

Dead generals and politicians standing, seated, riding, or laid out flat.

Alfred Gilbert, quoted in Richard Dorment, *Alfred Gilbert* (1986)

You have to give this much to the Luftwaffe – when it knocked down our buildings it didn't replace them with anything more offensive than rubble. We did that.

Prince Charles, speech to the Corporation of London Planning and Communications Committee, 2 December 1987

They Absolutely Love the Noise It Makes

The British may not like music, but they absolutely love the noise it makes.

Thomas Beecham, quoted in Howard Atkins and Archie Newman, *Beecham Stories* (1978)

What the English like is something they can beat time to, something that hits them straight on the drum of the ear.

George Frideric Handel, quoted in A. Schmid, *C.W. von Gluck* (1854)

English music? Did you say English music? Well, I've never heard of any!

Frederick Delius, quoted in Eric Fenby, *Delius as I Knew Him* (1936)

Much English music has the insipid flavour of the BBC Variety Orchestra playing an arrangement of a nursery tune.

Colin Wilson, *Brandy of the Damned* (1964)

English singers cannot sing. There is only one I know who can walk on the stage with any grace. The others come on like a duck in a thunderstorm.

Thomas Beecham, speech, Manchester Royal College of Music, 1914

These people have no ear, either for rhythm or music, and their unnatural passion for pianoforte playing and singing is thus all the more repulsive.

Heinrich Heine, *Lutezia* (1854)

Catford

Christ! I must be bored. I just thought of Catford.

Spike Milligan

Our best conductors ... usually reveal the Englishman's view that music is mainly a thing that can be whisked.

Neville Cardus, in the *Manchester Guardian*, 1939

Incomparably the Best Dull Writers

The English may not always be the best writers in the world, but they are incomparably the best dull writers.

Raymond Chandler, 'The Simple Art of Murder' (1944)

An Englishman never takes his collar off when he is writing. How can you expect him to show you his soul?

William McFee, *Harbours of Memory*, 'Reviewing Books' (1921)

To many, no doubt, he will seem to be somewhat blatant and bumptious, but we prefer to regard him as being simply British.

Oscar Wilde, book review in the *Pall Mall Gazette*, 18 November 1886

One should not be too severe on English novels; they are the only relaxation of the intellectually unemployed.

Oscar Wilde

England has the most sordid literary scene I've ever seen. They all meet in the same pub. This guy's writing a foreword for this person. They all have to give radio programs, they *have* to do all this just in order to scrape by. They're all scratching each other's backs.

William Burroughs, interviewed in 1980, quoted in Victor Bockris, *With William Burroughs: A Report from the Bunker* (1981)

A Series of Unpleasant Little Mews: The English Language

To learn English you must begin by thrusting the jaw forward, almost clenching the teeth, and practically immobilizing the lips. In this way the English produce the series of unpleasant little mews of which their language consists.

José Ortega y Gasset (1883–1955), Spanish philosopher and writer

The devil take these people and their language! They take a dozen monosyllabic words in their jaws, chew them, crunch them and spit them out again, and call that speaking. Fortunately they are by nature fairly silent, and although they gaze at us open-mouthed, they spare us long conversations.

Heinrich Heine

An Englishman's way of speaking absolutely
     classifies him.
The moment he talks he makes some other
     Englishman despise him.

Alan Jay Lerner, lyric from *My Fair Lady* (1956), adapting George Bernard Shaw's own preface to *Pygmalion* (1916): 'It is impossible for an Englishman to open his mouth without making some other Englishman hate him or despise him.'

We went to what is called in England 'an hotel'. If we could have afforded an horse and an hackney cab we could have had an heavenly time flitting around.

Mark Twain, in *Europe and Elsewhere* (ed. James Brander, 1923)

There is no such thing as 'the Queen's English'. The property has gone into the hands of a joint stock company and we own the bulk of the shares!

Mark Twain, *Following the Equator* (1897)

Foreigners pretend otherwise but if English is spoken loudly enough, anyone can understand it, the British included.

P.J. O'Rourke

Spit out the plum, to: To abandon an English accent.
Barry Humphries, Anglo-Australian glossary from *Bazza Pulls It Off* (1972)

The Food is More Dangerous than Sex

England is the only country where the food is more dangerous than sex.
Jackie Mason, *The World According to Me!* (1987)

Hell is a place where all the cooks are British.
Euro-joke, quoted in *Business Week*, 6 November 1995

Flesh-eaters, and insatiable of animal food; sottish and unrestrained in their appetites; full of suspicion.
Nicander Nucius of Corcyra, *Travels* (1545), on the English

In England there are sixty different religions, and only one sauce.
Francesco Caracciolo (1752–99), Neapolitan diplomat

The average cooking in the average hotel for the average Englishman explains to a large extent the English bleakness and taciturnity. Nobody can beam and warble while chewing pressed beef smeared with diabolical mustard. Nobody can exult aloud while ungluing from his teeth a quivering tapioca pudding.
Karel Čapek (1890–1938), Czech writer

Eat in most restaurants in England and pretty soon your head will no longer be on speaking terms with your stomach.
Kathy Lette, quoted in the *Observer*, 4 February 2001

To eat well in England, all you have to do is take breakfast three times a day.
W. Somerset Maugham, quoted in Ted Morgan, *Somerset Maugham* (1980)

'Turbot, Sir,' said the waiter, placing before me two fishbones, two eyeballs, and a bit of black mackintosh.
Thomas Earle Welby, *The Dinner Knell*, 'Birmingham or Crewe?' (1932)

It is possible to eat English piecrust, whatever you may think at first. The English eat it, and when they stand up and walk away, they are hardly bent over at all.
Margaret Halsey

Nearly every woman in England is competent to write an authoritative article on how not to cook cabbage.
Vyvyan Holland, *Wine and Food* (1935)

Boiled cabbage *à l'Anglaise* is something compared with which steamed coarse newsprint bought from bankrupt Finnish salvage dealers and heated over smoky oil stoves is an exquisite delicacy. Boiled British cabbage is something lower than ex-Army blankets stolen by dispossessed Goanese doss-housekeepers who used them to cover busted-down hen houses in the slum district of Karachi.
'Cassandra' (William Connor), in the *Daily Mirror*, 30 June 1950

From time immemorial, the English, saddled with a climate that produced nothing tastier than mangel-wurzels and suet, have been forced to import anything that would stay down for more than ten seconds.

Tony Hendra, 'EEC! It's the US of E!', in *National Lampoon*, 1976

The English contribution to world culture: the chip.

Kevin Kline as Otto, in the film *A Fish Called Wanda* (1988), screenplay by John Cleese and Charles Crichton

On the Continent people have good food; in England people have good table manners.

George Mikes, *How to be an Alien* (1946)

No wonder they were such a pasty lot. And so self-righteous about it, with their boundless contempt for garlic and messed-up foreign food with sauces. An exasperating people.

Alice Thomas Ellis, *The 27th Kingdom* (1982)

Pre-eminence in the Matter of Tea

English cuisine is so generally threadbare that for years there has been a gentlemen's agreement in the civilized world to allow the Brits pre-eminence in the matter of tea – which, after all, comes down to little more than the ability to boil water.

Wilfrid Sheed, 'Taking Pride in Prejudice', in *GQ*, 1984

The British have an umbilical cord which has never been cut and through which tea flows constantly. It is curious to watch them in times of sudden horror, tragedy or disaster. The pulse stops apparently, and nothing can be done, and no move made, until 'a nice cup of tea' is quickly made.

Marlene Dietrich, *Marlene Dietrich's ABC* (1984)

But certainly the tea is better than the coffee ...
English coffee tastes like water that has been squeezed out of a wet sleeve.

Fred Allen, *Treadmill to Oblivion* (1956)

Coffee in England is just toasted milk.

Christopher Fry, quoted in the *New York Post*, 1962

Best to stick to beer ... if you don't mind it warm:
What two ideas are more inseparable than Beer and Britannia?

Sydney Smith, quoted in Hesketh Pearson, *The Smith of Smiths* (1934)

England, where, indeed, they are most potent in potting: your Dane, your German, and your swag-bellied Hollander, are nothing to your English.

William Shakespeare, *Othello*, II.iii

Huntin', Shootin' an' Fishin'

The English country gentleman galloping after the fox – the unspeakable in full pursuit of the uneatable.

Oscar Wilde, *A Woman of No Importance* (1893)

Go anywhere in England where there are natural, wholesome, contented, and really nice English people; and what do you always find? That the stables are the real centre of the household ...

George Bernard Shaw, *Heartbreak House* (1919)

No sportsman wants to kill the fox or the pheasant as I want to kill him when I see him doing it.

George Bernard Shaw

The depressing thing about an Englishman's traditional love of animals is the dishonesty thereof – get a barbed hook into the upper lip of a salmon, drag him endlessly around the water until he loses his strength, pull him to the bank, hit him on the head with a stone, and you may well become fisherman of the year. Shoot the salmon and you'll never be asked again.

Clement Freud, *Freud on Food* (1978)

About one thing the Englishman has a particularly strict code. If a bird says *Cluk bik bik bik bik* and *caw* you may kill it, eat it or ask Fortnums to pickle it in Napoleon brandy with wild strawberries. If it says *tweet* it is a dear and precious friend and you'd better lay off it if you want to remain a member of Boodles.

Clement Freud, *Freud on Food* (1978)

Cricket: Baseball on Valium

Cricket is baseball on valium.
Robin Williams

It requires one to adopt such indecent postures.
Oscar Wilde, on his reluctance to play cricket

Personally, I have always looked on cricket as organized loafing.
Archbishop William Temple (1881–1944), remark to parents when headmaster at Repton

What Ashes?

Two disparaging Australian cricketing 'riddles' currently doing the rounds:
Q: **What is the height of optimism?**
A: **An English batsman applying sunblock cream.**

Q: **What do you call an Englishman with 100 runs against his name?**
A: **A test bowler.**

And finally... a piece of 'sledging':
Australian bowler to any English batsman:
Q: **What's the difference between a pom and a bucket of shit?**
A: **The bucket, dickhead.**

Many continentals think life is a game. The English think cricket is a game.

George Mikes, *How to be an Alien* (1946)

I have seen cricket, and I know it isn't true.

Danny Kaye

Cricket is the only game that you can actually put on weight when playing.

Tommy Docherty, Scottish football manager

Oh God, if there be cricket in heaven, let there also be rain.

Alec Douglas Home, 'Prayer of a Cricketer's Wife'

Cricket is a game which the British, not being a spiritual people, had to invent in order to have some concept of eternity.

Lord Mancroft, *Bees in Some Bonnets* (1979)

Soccer: What Athlete's Foot is to Injuries

Soccer is to sport what athlete's foot is to injuries.

Tom Weir, US sportswriter, in *USA Today*

Football – proper football – is British in origin, and thus attracts the derision of Americans:

There's a good reason why you don't care about soccer – it's because you are an American and hating soccer is more American than mom's apple pie, driving a pick-up and spending Saturday afternoon channel-surfing with the remote control.

Tom Weir, in *USA Today*

Soccer is a game in which everyone does a lot of running around. Twenty-one guys stand around and one guy does a tap dance with the ball. It's about as exciting as *Tristan and Isolde*.

Jim Murray, US sportswriter, in the *Los Angeles Times*, 1967

Liverpool

The folk that live in Liverpool, their heart is in
    their boots;
They go to hell like lambs, they do, because the
    hooter hoots.

G.K. Chesterton, 'Me Heart'

In your Liverpool slums, in your Liverpool slums,
You look in the dustbin for something to eat,
You find a dead rat and you think it's a treat,
In your Liverpool slums.

English football song, aimed at fans of Liverpool FC, sung to the tune 'My Liverpool Home', 1980

Wales: My Fathers Can Have It

The land of my fathers – my fathers can have it.
Dylan Thomas, quoted in *Adam* magazine, December 1953.
'Land of My Fathers' is the Welsh national anthem, written in
1856 by Evan James and translated by W.G. Rothery.

Leeks and Taffs

Wales was formerly known as *Itchland* (for similar reasons that
Scotland was known as *Louseland* or *Scratchland*), and was
also dismissively termed *Leekshire*. The Welsh were once
known as *Leeks* or *Welsh goats*, while *Welshies*, *Taffies* (from
Dafydd, the Welsh form of David) and *Taffs* are still current. *Taffs*
gave rise to the rhyming slang *Riff-raffs*, and to the *Taffia*, the
collective noun for the movers and shakers of modern Wales.

An Impotent People, Sick with Inbreeding

An impotent people,
Sick with inbreeding,
Worrying the carcase of an old song.
R.S. Thomas, 'Welsh Landscape' (1955)

The Welsh are a nation of male-voice choir lovers
whose only hobbies are rugby and romantic
involvement with sheep.
Lenny Henry, comedian

Gloomy, Mountainous and Green

Wales, which I have never seen,
Is gloomy, mountainous, and green,
And, as I judge from reading Borrow,
The people there rejoice in sorrow ...
The weather veers from dull to foul,
The letter W's a vowel.

Rolfe Humphries, American poet, 'For My Ancestors', in
Collected Poems (1965)

The Welsh are not meant to go out in the sun. They
start to photosynthesize.

Rhys Ifans

Each section of the British Isles has its own way of
laughing, except Wales, which doesn't.

Stephen Leacock

There are still parts of Wales where the only
concession to gaiety is a striped shroud.

Gwyn Thomas, in *Punch*, 18 June 1958

What are they *for*?

Anne Robinson, consigning the Welsh to Room 101, in the
eponymous BBC TV programme, March 2001. Robinson also
described the Welsh as 'irritating and annoying', adding, 'They
are always so pleased with themselves.' The comments
aroused fury and accusations of racism from Welsh MPs.

It is because of their sins, and more particularly the wicked and detestable vice of homosexuality, that the Welsh were punished by God and so lost first Troy and then Britain.

Gerald of Wales (aka Giraldus Cambrensis), *The Description of Wales* (*c.* 1194)

The Welsh are the Italians in the rain.

Anonymous

When all else fails
try Wales.

Christopher Logue, 'To a Friend in Search of Rural Seclusion'

Totally Vile and Worthless: English Antipathy

The earth contains no race of human beings so totally vile and worthless as the Welsh.

Walter Savage Landor, letter to Robert Southey

The older the Welshman, the more a madman.

English saying

Now I perceive the devil understands Welsh.

William Shakespeare, *Henry IV, Part 1*, III.i

Hence! I am qualmish at the smell of leek.

Pistol to Fluellen, in William Shakespeare, *Henry V*, V.i

The Welsh are so damn Welsh that it looks like affectation.

Walter Raleigh (1861–1922), letter to D.B. Wyndham Lewis

'We can trace almost all the disasters of English history to the influence of Wales.' ... 'The Welsh,' said the Doctor, 'are the only nation in the world that has produced no graphic or plastic art, no architecture, no drama. They just sing,' he said with disgust, 'sing and blow down wind instruments of plated silver.'

Dr Fagan, in Evelyn Waugh's *Decline and Fall* (1928)

It profits a man nothing to give his soul for the whole world ... But for Wales – !

Robert Bolt, *A Man for All Seasons* (1960)

Eddy was a tremendously tolerant person, but he wouldn't put up with the Welsh. He always said, surely there's enough English to go round.

John Mortimer, *Two Stars for Comfort* (1962)

The Welshman's dishonest, he cheats when
   he can,
And little and dark – more like monkey than man.
He works underground with a lamp in his hat,
And he sings far too loud, far too often, and flat.

Michael Flanders (with Donald Swann), 'A Song of Patriotic Prejudice', from *At the Drop of Another Hat* (1963)

Finding out that your sister is black is fine; finding out that your sister is Welsh is another thing.

A.A. Gill

Taffy was a Thief

**Taffy was a Welshman, Taffy was a thief,
Taffy came into my house and stole a side of beef.**
Part of an English nursery rhyme

**They are treacherous to each other as well as to
foreigners, covet freedom, neglect peace, are warlike
and skilful in arms, and are eager for revenge.**
Walter Map (1140–1209), English writer

**The Welsh peasants have the reputation ... of being
singularly false and never speaking their minds ... If
this be true, they are worthy descendants of their
countrymen of old, who betrayed their chiefs, and
those chiefs each other.**
Louisa Costello, *Falls, Lakes, and Mountains in North Wales* (1845)

Here be Dragons

Welsh women appear to have been a particular
target of English disdain:
**The ordinary women of Wales are generally
short and squat, ill-favoured and nasty.**
David Mallet (1705–65), letter to Alexander Pope

**Welshmen prize their women so highly that
they put a picture of their mother-in-law on
the national flag.**
Anonymous. The symbol on the Welsh flag is, of
course, a dragon.

A Welshman is a man who prays on his knees on Sundays and preys on his neighbours all the rest of the week.
Anonymous

The Welsh are all actors. It's only the bad ones who become professionals.
Richard Burton, quoted in the *Listener*, 9 January 1986

Finally, a regrettable outburst regarding Welsh Labour councillors:
They're all the same. They're short, they're fat, they're slimy and they're fundamentally corrupt.
Rod Richards, junior minister at the Welsh Office in John Major's Conservative government, December 1994

The Land of Song, but No Music

Wales is the land of song, but no music.
David Wulstan

LADY PERCY: Lie still, ye thief, and hear the lady sing in Welsh.
HOTSPUR: I had rather hear Lady my brach howl in Irish.
William Shakespeare, *Henry IV, Part 1*, III.i

Here I am in Wales ... a harpist sits in the lobby of every inn of repute playing so-called folk melodies at you – i.e. dreadful, vulgar, fake stuff, and *simultaneously* a hurdy-gurdy is tootling out melodies ... it's even given me a toothache.
Felix Mendelssohn, in a letter to his teacher, Zelter, from Llangollen, 8 August 1829

It is strange that, though they will burst into song on no provocation at all, the Welsh have produced so few eminent composers – with, of course, the exception of Johann Sebastian Bach.

Anonymous, quoted in Leslie Ayre, *The Wit of Music* (1966)

The Welsh are such good singers because they have no locks on their bathroom doors.

Harry Secombe (1921–2001)

Welsh Rarebit

... there was in heaven a great company of Welshmen which with their cracking and babbling troubled all the others. Wherefore God said to Saint Peter that He was weary of them and that He would fain have them out of heaven. ...

Wherefore Saint Peter went out of heaven-gates and cried with a loud voice, 'Caws pob' – that is as much to say 'roasted cheese' – which thing the Welshmen hearing, ran out of heaven a great pace. And when Saint Peter saw them all out, he suddenly went into heaven and locked the door ...

Anonymous, *Merry Tales, Wittie Questions and Quicke Answers* (1567)

Scotland the What?

Scotland has gone by a variety of names. In the 17th century it was *Louseland*, which began to give way to *Scratchland* in the 18th century (Wales was *Itchland*). The causes of the scratching were known as *Scots greys* or simply *Scotchmen*. The lack of hygiene found by visitors is reflected in another slang term, *Scotch lick*, a poorly performed cleaning job.

General antipathy is reflected in the term *Scotch fiddle* for venereal disease (18th–19th centuries); *to play the Scotch fiddle* was to rub the index finger of one hand between the index finger and thumb of the other hand, a gesture implying to a Scotsman that he suffered from the affliction.

By the late 19th century Scotland appears to have cleaned up its act, and became known as *Haggisland* or *Marmalade Country*. The term *North Britain*, coined after the Union with England of 1707, never really caught on.

The Scots themselves are *Scotchies*, *Jocks* or, via rhyming slang, *Sweaty Socks*. A recent innovation is the unpleasant *Porridge Wogs*, while the confused Antipodeans refer to the Scots – rather than the inhabitants of Newcastle – as *Geordies*.

A Very Vile Country

So said Samuel Johnson. Indeed, he had so many rude things to say about Scots and Scotland that we have a whole section below devoted to his diatribes. But first, some other hostile voices – mostly, but not exclusively, English:

**The Scotsman is mean, as we're all well aware,
And bony, and blotchy, and covered with hair,
He eats salted porridge, he works all the day,
And he hasn't got Bishops to show him the way.**
Michael Flanders (with Donald Swann), 'A Song of Patriotic Prejudice', from *At the Drop of Another Hat* (1963)

As hard-hearted as a Scot of Scotland.
English saying

**Had Cain been Scot, God would have changed his doom
Not forced him wander, but confined him home.**
John Cleveland (1613–58), 'The Rebel Scot'

In all my travels I never met with any one Scotchman but what was a man of sense: I believe everybody of that country that has any, leaves it as fast as they can.
Francis Lockier (1668–1740), English churchman and writer, quoted in Joseph Spence, *Anecdotes* (1820)

**A land of meanness, sophistry and mist.
Each breeze from foggy mount and marshy plain
Dilutes with drivel every drizzly brain.**
Lord Byron, 'The Curse of Minerva' (1812)

I have been trying all my life to like Scotchmen, and am obliged to desist from the experiment in despair.
Charles Lamb, *The Essays of Elia*, 'Imperfect Sympathies' (1820–23)

In every corner of the world you will find a Scot, a rat, and a Newcastle grindstone.

Old saying, quoted in John Gibson Lockhart, *Memoirs of the Life of Sir Walter Scott* (1837–8)

He is the fine gentleman whose father toils with a muck-fork ... He is the bandy-legged lout from Tullietudlescleugh, who, after a childhood of intimacy with the cesspool and the crab louse, and twelve months at 'the college' on moneys wrung from the diet of his family, drops his threadbare kilt and comes south in a slop suit to instruct the English in the arts of civilization and in the English language.

T.W.H. Crosland, *The Unspeakable Scot* (1902)

The Auld Alliance Turns Sour

If a Frenchman goes on about seagulls, trawlers and sardines, he's called a philosopher. I'd just be called a short Scottish bum talking crap.

Gordon Strachan, Scottish footballer, referring to Eric Cantona in 1995

There are few more impressive sights in the world than a Scotsman on the make.

J.M. Barrie, *What Every Woman Knows* (1908)

A Worse England: Dr Johnson's Bête Noire

Seeing Scotland, Madam, is only seeing a worse England. It is seeing the flower fade away to the naked stalk.
Samuel Johnson, quoted in James Boswell, *The Life of Samuel Johnson* (1791). All except for the last quotation in this section are from the same source; Boswell, a Scot, gleefully recorded his friend's barbs.

God made it, but we must remember that He made it for Scotchmen; and comparisons are odious, but God made Hell.

Much ... may be made of a Scotchman, if he be *caught* young.

Their learning is like bread in a besieged town: every man gets a little, but no man gets a full meal.

You've forgotten the greatest moral attribute of a Scotsman, Maggie, that he'll do nothing which might damage his career.
J.M. Barrie, *What Every Woman Knows* (1908)

***Racial characteristics*: sour, stingy, depressing beggars who parade around in schoolgirls' skirts with nothing on underneath. Their fumbled attempt at speaking the**

Sir, let me tell you, the noblest prospect which a Scotchman ever sees is the high road that leads him to England.

BOSWELL: I do indeed come from Scotland, but I cannot help it ...

JOHNSON: That, Sir, I find, is what a very great many of your countrymen cannot help.

Sir, it is not so much to be lamented that Old England is lost, as that the Scotch have found it.

Of an inn at Bristol:
Describe it, Sir? – Why, it was so bad that Boswell wished to be in Scotland.

English language has been a source of amusement for five centuries, and their idiot music has been dreaded by those not blessed with deafness for at least as long.
P.J. O'Rourke, 'Foreigners Around the World', in *National Lampoon*, 1976

Nobody knows what the original people of Scotland were: cold is probably the best informed guess, and wet.
A.A. Gill

We're ruled by effete arseholes. What does that make us? The lowest of the fuckin low, the scum of the earth. The most wretched, servile, miserable pathetic trash that was ever shat intae creation. Ah don't hate the English. They just git oan wi the shite thuv goat. Ah hate the Scots.

Renton, in Irvine Welsh's *Trainspotting* (1993)

A Virtue Called Thrift

The vice of meanness, condemned in every other country, is in Scotland translated into a virtue called 'thrift'.

David Thomson, *Nairn in Darkness and Light* (1987)

No McTavish
Was ever lavish.

Ogden Nash, 'Genealogical Reflection', *Hard Lines* (1931)

A Scotsman returns from London:
Mun, a had na' been the-ere abune twa hoours when – *Bang* – went *Saxpence!*

Birket Foster, caption for a Charles Keene cartoon in *Punch*, 5 December 1868. Foster got the joke from John Gilbert.

Three failures and a fire make a Scotsman's fortune.

Scottish saying

Scotsmen take all they can get – and a little more, if they can.

Scottish saying

The Scotsman is one who keeps the Sabbath and everything else he can lay his hands on.
American saying

Jews, Scotsmen and counterfeits will be encountered throughout the world.
German saying

I think it possible that all Scots are illegitimate, Scotsmen being so mean and Scotswomen so generous.
Edwin Muir, Orkney-born poet

Auld Reekie

Edinburgh is fondly known by its inhabitants as 'Auld Reekie' (= old smoky) or more pretentiously as 'the Athens of the North'. However, some have preferred to see it as:

The Reykjavik of the South.
Tom Stoppard, *Jumpers* (1972)

**The bitter east, the misty summer
And grey metropolis of the North.**
Alfred, Lord Tennyson, 'The Daisy' (1847)

You can have more fun at a Glasgow funeral than at an Edinburgh wedding.
Anonymous

'The Dear Green Place'

Some blind person must have dreamt up this as a name for Glasgow, as

The great thing about Glasgow now is that if there's a nuclear attack, it'll look exactly the same afterwards.

Billy Connolly, *Gullible's Travels*, 'Scotland' (1982)

When Adam Smith, the Glaswegian economist, was boasting about the charms of Glasgow to Dr Johnson, the latter responded:

Pray, Sir, have you ever seen Brentford?

Quoted in James Boswell, *The Life of Samuel Johnson* (1791)

Glasgow is renowned for three things in particular:

Sectarian fervour ...

A Glaswegian atheist is a bloke who goes to a Rangers–Celtic match to watch the football.

Sandy Strang

World-class drinking ...

A Glaswegian was spotted by his minister leaving a pub. 'Tut, tut,' says the minister, 'and I thought you were a teetotaller.'

'Aye, I am, minister, but no' a bigoted wan.'

Old joke

And unresponsive audiences ... for example, when someone mentioned to Ken Dodd the theory of Freud that jokes result in elation and relief from tension, he responded:

The trouble with Freud is that he never played the Glasgow Empire Saturday night.

There are of course endless jokes about Scottish thriftiness ... but w'ur no prepared ti gie ye mair than a wee smidgen:

A waiter notices that a Scotsman has a fly in his soup. 'Shall I bring you a fresh bowl, sir?'

'No,' says the Scotsman, picking the fly out of his soup and shaking it. 'Come oan, spit it oot, ya wee bastard!'

q: **What's the difference between a Scotsman and a canoe?**

a: **A Scotsman doesn't tip.**

After a typically meagre collection during the Sunday service the minister prays, 'We thank thee, Lord, that the plate was returned safely.' On another occasion the minister requests that the congregation at least donate their *own* buttons, and not to take those from the cushions on the pews.

Did you hear about the Scottish smash-and-grab robber who got arrested when he went back to the jewellers for the brick?

And that's all the Mean Scotsman jokes you're going to get out of us. But as compensation here are some slang expressions deriving from the same stereotype. A *Scotsman's grandstand* is a vantage point from which a sporting event may be viewed for free, and in the 1930s Piccadilly Circus was known as the *Scotsman's cinema*. In New Zealand a *Scotsman's shout* is a round where everybody buys their own drinks, while a *Scotch screw* is a nocturnal emission – free, and not given to anyone else.

Dour Scots: Calvin, Knox and Sulphur

**That garret of the earth – that knuckle-end of England
– that land of Calvin, oatcakes and sulphur.**

Sydney Smith, quoted in Lady Holland, *A Memoir of Sydney Smith* (1855)

**O Knox he was a bad man
he split the Scottish mind.
The one half he made cruel
and the other half unkind.**

Alan Jackson (1938–). Calvin and Knox are, it seems, largely to
blame for the dourness of the Scots – 'this preposterous
Presbyterian breed', as Hugh MacDiarmid described them.
'The history of Scotland', Ivor Brown once observed, 'is one of
theology tempered by homicide.'

Indeed, the Scots have provided the international benchmark
for dourness in matters of religion:

**Lutherans are like Scottish people, only with less
frivolity.**

Garrison Keillor, quoted in the *Independent*, 1992

**The whole nation hitherto has been void of wit and
humour, and even incapable of relishing it.**

Horace Walpole, letter to Sir Horace Mann, 1778

**It requires a surgical operation to get a joke well into a
Scotch understanding.**

Sydney Smith, quoted in Lady Holland, *A Memoir of Sydney
Smith* (1855). When this is quoted to a Scotsman in J.M.

Barrie's play *What Every Woman Knows*, the said
Scotsman replies: 'What beats me, Maggie, is how you
could insert a joke with an operation.'

**It is never difficult to distinguish between a
Scotsman with a grievance and a ray of sunshine.**
P.G. Wodehouse, *Blandings Castle and Elsewhere*, 'The
Custody of the Pumpkin' (1935)

Bitin' and scratchin' is Scotch folks' wooing.
John Rae, *Proverbs* (1670)

On coming across a gibbet in an uncharted part of Africa:
**The sight of it gave me infinite pleasure, as it
proved that I was in a civilized society.**
Mungo Park, Scottish explorer, *Travels in the Interior
Districts of Africa* (1797)

**While swordless Scotland, sadder than
    its psalms,
Fosters its sober youth on national alms
To breed a dull provincial discipline,
Commerce its god and golf its anodyne.**
Eric Linklater, 'Preamble to a Satire'

**The Irish are great talkers
Persuasive and disarming,
You can say lots and lots
Against the Scots –
But at least they're never charming!**
Gavin Ewart, *The Complete Little Ones* (1986)

Kilts and Bagpipes Come Awa'

Highlanders, or *Teuchters* as they are pejoratively known by the Lowland Scots, are often mocked for their cultural appurtenances.

Join a Highland regiment, my boy. The kilt is an unrivalled garment for fornication and diarrhoea.
John Masters, *Bugles and a Tiger* (1956)

When a lady asked a Highlander what was worn under the kilt he replied, 'Nothin', it's a' in purrfect workin' order.'
Very old joke

The best place to listen to bagpipes being played in Scotland is London.
Anonymous

A true gentleman is a man who knows how to play the bagpipes – but doesn't.
Anonymous

Scots Wedding Customs

For a marriage to be valid in Scotland it is absolutely necessary that it should be consummated in the presence of two policemen.
Samuel Butler (1835–1902)

Glaswegian Graffito

Drink is your enemy.
Love your enemy.
Juxtaposed graffiti allegedly spotted in Glasgow

The bagpipes sound exactly the same when you have finished learning them as when you start.
Sir Thomas Beecham

I got to try the bagpipes. It was like trying to blow an octopus.
James Galway, *An Autobiography* (1978)

The missing link between music and noise.
Des MacHale, *The Tiny Book of Scottish Jokes* (1988)

In the Land of the Deep-Fried Mars Bar

Drink being so important in Scotland, food definitely takes second place.

Queen Victoria had a bleak experience of Scottish catering at an inn at Dalwhinnie:
Unfortunately there was hardly anything to eat, and there was only tea, and two miserable starved Highland chickens, without any potatoes! No pudding, and no fun!
Journal, 8 October 1861

The chickens were doubtless a shocking indulgence, porridge being the staple fare of the natives:

***Oats*: A grain which in England is generally given to horses, but in Scotland supports the people.**

Samuel Johnson, *A Dictionary of the English Language* (1755)

More luxuriously, there is what Burns called the 'chieftain of the pudding race' (although sheep's guts mixed with barley was probably not what Victoria had in mind when she bemoaned the absence of pudding at Dalwhinnie):

**One often yearns
For the land of Burns –
The only snag is
The haggis!**

Lils Emslie, *Other People's Clerihews* (1983)

The Morals of Old Aberdeen

**Here lie the bones of Elizabeth Charlotte,
That was born a virgin and died a harlot.
She was aye a virgin till seventeen –
An extraordinary thing for Aberdeen.**

Alleged epitaph, quoted in Donald and Catherine Carswell's, *The Scots Week-End* (1936)

Ireland the Impossible

Ireland is a country in which the probable never happens and the impossible always does.
John Pentland Mahaffy (1839–1919), Irish scholar

Paddies, Micks, Shovels and Picks

Ireland is variously known as *Paddyland*, *Murphyland* and *Patland*, and the Irish as *Pats*, *Paddies* and *Micks*, hence also the rhyming slang *Shovel and Picks*. They have also been called *Boghoppers*, *Boglanders* and *Bogtrotters*. At one time they were also called *Teaguelanders*, from *Teague*, a Catholic. A recent innovation for a particular brand of Irishman is *Nipplie* – New Irish Patriot Permanently Living In Exile.

A lot of slang derives from various aspects of national stereotyping. For example:

Stupidity: *paddy and mick*, stupid (rhyming slang for thick); *Irish hint*, a very broad hint; *Irish hurricane*, a flat calm; *Irish screwdriver*, a hammer.

Poverty: *Irish* or *paddy's apple* or *Irish football* or *grape*, a potato; *paddy's eyewater*, illegally distilled whiskey; *paddy's lantern*, the moon (1930s, from the lack of electricity in rural Ireland); *paddy's market*, a market selling cheap goods; *Irish baby buggy* or *ambulance* or *chariot*, a wheelbarrow; *Irish draperies*, cobwebs.

Temper and violence: *Irish*, temper (US); *paddywhack*, a violent beating or an outburst of temper; *Irish confetti*, bricks, as thrown in a fight; *Irish wedding*, a brawl; *Irish hoist*, a kick up the backside; *Irishman's coat of arms*, a black eye.

A Perverse and Complex People

An Irishman is a guy who:
Believes everything he can't see, and nothing he can.
Has such great respect for the truth, he only uses
it in emergencies.
Can lick any man in the house he is the sole occupant of.
Believes salvation can be achieved by means of a
weekly envelope ...
We are a very perverse, complex people. It's what
makes us loveable. We're banking heavily that God
has a sense of humour.

Jim Murray, in the *Los Angeles Times*, 1976

Of my Nation! What ish my Nation? Ish a villain, and a
bastard, and a knave and a rascal.

Macmorris, in William Shakespeare's *Henry V*, III.ii

A servile race in folly nursed,
Who truckle most when treated worst.

Jonathan Swift (1667–1745)

The Irish ... are the damnedest race. They put so much
emphasis on so many wrong things.

Rhett 'I-don't-give-a-damn' Butler, in Margaret Mitchell's *Gone with the Wind* (1936)

Other people have a nationality. The Irish and the Jews have a psychosis.

Brendan Behan, *Richard's Cork Leg* (1972)

Charming, soft-voiced, quarrelsome, priest-ridden, feckless and happily devoid of the slightest integrity in our stodgy English sense of the word.

Noël Coward, *Diary*, 1960

Jesus must have been an Irishman. After all, He was unmarried, thirty-two years old, lived at home, and His mother thought He was God.

Shane Connaughton, *Divisions at the Oscar*

The sex urge in Ireland is either sublimated by religion, dissipated in sport or drowned in drink, or in the case of Paddy Kavanagh, all three.

Niall Toibin

The Irish are often nervous about having the appropriate face for the occasion. They have to be happy at weddings, which is a strain, so they get depressed; they have to be sad at funerals, which is easy, so they get happy.

Peggy Noonan, *What I Saw at the Revolution* (1990)

Thick ... Legs

As to the natural history of the Irish species, they are only remarkable for the thickness of their legs, especially those of plebeian females.

Richard Twiss, *Tour in Ireland* (1776)

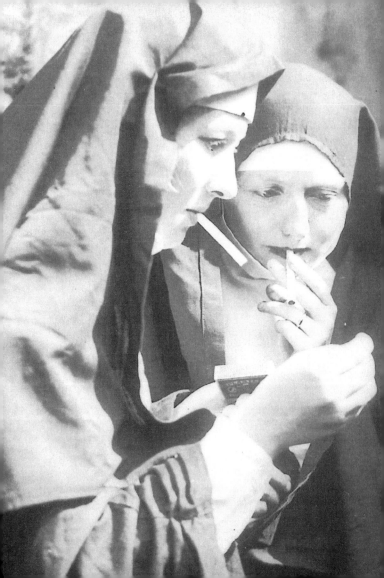

Behaving Like a Lavatory Attendant: Ireland Today

Ireland is a modern nation but it is modernized only recently and at the moment it is behaving rather like a lavatory attendant who has just won the lottery.

Terry Eagleton

Ireland, the *Big Issue* seller of Europe.

A.A. Gill

The Irish don't know what they want and are prepared to fight to the death to get it.

Sydney Littlewood, speech, 13 April 1961

Home and Away

I reckon no man is thoroughly miserable unless he be condemn'd to live in Ireland.

Jonathan Swift, letter to Ambrose Philips, 1709

A beautiful country, sir, to live out of!

Thomas Moore (1779–1852)

Among the countless blessings I thank God for, my failure to find a house in Ireland comes first ... The peasants are malevolent. All their smiles are false as hell. Their priests are very suitable for them but not for foreigners. No coal at all. Awful incompetence everywhere. No native capable of doing the simplest job.

Evelyn Waugh, letter to Nancy Mitford, 1 May 1952

Men have been dying for Ireland since the beginning of time and look at the state of the country.
Frank McCourt, *Angela's Ashes* (1996)

Rumour has it that the Aran Islands are rolled up when the tourist season ends and towed into Galway, where workmen chip away at the rocks to make them look a bit more rugged.
Terry Eagleton

John Bull's Other Island: Ireland and the English
John Bull's Other Island was the title of a 1904 play by George Bernard Shaw.

Now for our Irish wars:
We must supplant those rough rug-headed kerns,
Which live like venom where no venom else
But only they have privilege to live.
William Shakespeare, *Richard II*, II.i ('kern' = lightly armed Irish foot soldier)

Hang the harpers wherever found.
Elizabeth I, proclamation of 1603

The moment the very name of Ireland is mentioned, the English seem to bid adieu to common feeling, common prudence, and to common sense, and to act with the barbarity of tyrants, and the fatuity of idiots.
Sydney Smith, *Letters of Peter Plymley* (1807)

The Irish militia are useless in times of war and dangerous in times of peace.

The Duke of Wellington

The Irish seem to me like a pack of hounds, always dragging down some noble stag.

Johann Wolfgang von Goethe, speaking in support of the Duke of Wellington's opposition to Catholic Emancipation

So great and so long has been the misgovernment of Ireland, that we verily believe the empire would be much stronger if every thing was open sea between England and the Atlantic, and if skates and cod-fish swam over the fair land of Ulster.

Sydney Smith, in the *Edinburgh Review*, 1820

The only way to deal with such a man as O'Connell is to hang him up and erect a statue to him under the gallows.

Sydney Smith, quoted in Hesketh Pearson, *The Smith of Smiths* (1934). The Irish patriot Daniel O'Connell (1775–1847) was known as 'the Liberator'.

**Scum condensed of Irish bog,
Ruffian, coward, demagogue,
Boundless liar, base detractor,
Nurse of murders, treason factor.**

Anonymous broadside against Daniel O'Connell in *The Times*

The bane of England, and the opprobrium of Europe.

Benjamin Disraeli, speech, 9 August 1843, referring to Ireland

The Irish What?

Consider Ireland. ... You have a starving population, an absentee aristocracy, and an alien Church, and in addition the weakest executive in the world. That is the 'Irish Question'.

Benjamin Disraeli, speech to the House of Commons, 16 February 1844

Proposed solution to the Irish Question:
You've got to exchange the populations of Holland and Ireland. Then the Dutch will turn Ireland into a beautiful garden and the Irish will forget to mend the dikes and will all be drowned.

Otto von Bismarck

Gladstone ... spent his declining years trying to guess the answer to the Irish Question; unfortunately, whenever he was getting warm, the Irish secretly changed the Question.

W.C. Sellar and R.J. Yeatman, *1066 and All That* (1930)

I never met anyone in Ireland who understood the Irish question, except one Englishman who had only been there a week.

Major Sir Keith Fraser MP, remark, 1919

The whole figures in my mind like a ragged coat, one huge beggar's gaberdine, not patched, nor patchable any longer.

Thomas Carlyle, *Journal*, 11 November 1849

The Irish are difficult to deal with. For one thing the English do not understand their innate love of fighting and blows. If on either side of an Irishman's road to Paradise shillelahs grew, which automatically hit him on the head, yet he would not be satisfied.

Alfred, Lord Tennyson, quoted in *Alfred, Lord Tennyson: A Memoir* (1897)

The Venice of Ireland

We have often heard Cork called the Venice of Ireland, but have never heard Venice called the Cork of Italy.

Anonymous, quoted by John Betjeman in a letter to Michael Rose, 25 September 1955

The English and the Irish are very much alike, except that the Irish are more so.

Monsignor James Dunne (1859–1934), remark during the first Troubles

There is no topic ... more soporific and generally boring than the topic of Ireland *as Ireland, as a nation.*

Ezra Pound, in *New Age*, 8 January 1920

If, in the eyes of an Irishman, there is anyone being more ridiculous than an Englishman, it is an Englishman who loves Ireland.

André Maurois, *Ariel* (1923)

'You disapprove of the Swedes?'
'Yes, sir.'
'Why?'
'Their heads are too square, sir.'
'And you disapprove of the Irish?'
'Yes, sir.'
'Why?'
'Because they are Irish, sir.'

P.G. Wodehouse, *The Small Bachelor* (1927)

PAT: He was an Anglo-Irishman.
MEG: In the blessed name of God what's that?
PAT: A Protestant with a horse.

Brendan Behan, *The Hostage* (1958)

The Irishman, now, our contempt is beneath –
He sleeps in his boots and he lies in his teeth.
He blows up policemen, or so I have heard,
And blames it on Cromwell and William the Third.

Michael Flanders (with Donald Swann), 'A Song of Patriotic Prejudice', from *At the Drop of Another Hat* (1963)

Chloroform and Hashish: Irish Politics

Politics is the chloroform of the Irish people, or rather the hashish.

Oliver St John Gogarty, *As I Was Going Down Sackville Street* (1937)

Our ancestors believed in magic, prayers, trickery, browbeating and bullying: I think it would be fair to sum that list up as 'Irish politics'.

Flann O'Brien, in Kevin O'Noland (ed.), *The Hair of the Dogma* (1977)

Every party in Ireland was founded on the gun.

John Hume, remark, 1995

Domestic Hate

Hapless Nation! hapless Land
Heap of uncementing sand!
Crumbled by a foreign weight:
And by worse, domestic hate.

William Drennan, 'The Wake of William Orr' (1797)

The Irish are a fair people; they never speak well of one another.

Samuel Johnson, 18 February 1775, quoted in James Boswell, *Life of Samuel Johnson* (1791)

History of Ireland – lawlessness and turbulency, robbery and oppression, hatred and revenge, blind

selfishness everywhere – no principle, no heroism. What can be done with it?

William Allingham, *Diary*, 11 November 1866

Ireland is the old sow that eats her farrow.

Stephen Dedalus in James Joyce's *A Portrait of the Artist as a Young Man* (1916)

Put an Irishman on the spit, and you can always get another Irishman to turn him.

George Bernard Shaw

Dublin's Fair City

This town [Dublin] ... I believe is the most disagreeable place in Europe, at least to any but those who have been accustomed to it from their youth, and in such a case I suppose a jail might be tolerable.

Jonathan Swift, letter to Knightly Chetwode, 23 November 1727

Dublin, that city of tedious and silly derision.

George Bernard Shaw, 1911

I gave him a Dublin uppercut – a kick in the groin.

Brendan Behan

The Irish are the niggers of Europe ... An' Dubliners are the niggers of Ireland ... An' the northside Dubliners are the niggers o' Dublin – Say it loud. I'm black an' I'm proud.

Roddy Doyle, *The Commitments* (1987)

Born in a Stable

Because a man is born in a stable that does not make him a horse.

The Duke of Wellington, who was born in Ireland

To marry the Irish is to look for poverty.

J.P. Donleavy, *The Ginger Man* (1955)

My grandmother took a bath every year, whether she was dirty or not.

Brendan Behan, *Brendan Behan's Island* (1962)

Have you heard about the Irishman who had a leg transplant? His welly rejected it.

Frank Carson

The Irish do not want anyone to wish them well; they want everyone to wish their enemies ill.

Harold Nicolson

**... Ireland, a nation
Built upon violence and morose vendettas.**

Louis MacNeice, *Eclogue From Ireland* (1936)

Nobody can betray Ireland: it does not give him the chance; it betrays him first.

Oliver St John Gogarty, *As I Was Going Down Sackville Street* (1937)

Loving and Fighting

**Where there are Irish there's loving and fighting,
And when we stop either, it's Ireland no more!**
Rudyard Kipling, 'The Irish Guards' (1918)

**They do nothing in Ireland as they would elsewhere.
When the Dublin mail was stopped and robbed my
brother declares that a sweet female voice was heard
behind the hedge, exclaiming, 'Shoot the gintlemman,
then, Patrick dear.'**
Sydney Smith, quoted in Lady Holland, *Memoir of Sydney Smith* (1855)

**For the great Gaels of Ireland
Are the men that God made mad,
For all their wars are merry
And all their songs are sad.**
G.K. Chesterton, *The Ballad of the White Horse* (1911)

The Irishman is never at peace except when he is fighting.
Irish saying

Potatoes into Human Nature

Every Irishman has a potato in his head.
J.C. and A.W. Hare, *Guesses at Truth* (1827)

**What is an Irishman but a mere machine for
converting potatoes into human nature.**
Edward Vaughan Kenealy, *Table-Talk* (1875)

Not Suffering Common Sense

The Irish people do not gladly suffer common sense.
Oliver St John Gogarty, in 1935

An Englishman thinks seated; a Frenchman, standing; an American pacing; an Irishman afterward.
Austin O'Malley (1858–1932)

'Verbal agreements,' said the Irish attorney, 'are not worth the paper they are written on.'
J.C. Percy, *Bulls Ancient and Modern* (1912) – predating the famous Goldwynism

Sure, the next train has gone ten minutes ago.
Anonymous cartoon in *Punch*, 20 May 1871

Sure God help the Irish, if it was raining soup, they'd be out with forks.
Brendan Behan, *Brendan Behan's Island* (1962)

An Irish homosexual is one who prefers women to drink.
Sean Ó'Faoláin

Cleanliness is next to Godliness – only in an Irish dictionary.
Graffito

Knocking down a house in Dublin recently, the workmen found a skeleton with a medal on a ribbon around its neck. The inscription was: Irish Hide and Seek Champion 1910.
Frank Carson

Paddy wrote a letter to his Irish Molly O',
Saying 'Should you not receive it, write and let me
   know.'

Jack Judge and Harry Williams, 'Tipperary' (1912)

Seamus and Sean start work at a sawmill. After an hour
Seamus lets out a big yell.
'Help, Sean, I lost me finger!'
'Now how did you go about doing that?'
'Sure I just touched the big spinning job here, just like
   thi— Feck! There goes another one.'

Internet joke

Seamus phones the airline to find out how long it takes
to fly from Boston to Dublin.
'Er, just a minute, sir ...' says the man at the airline.
'Jasus, that's fast. Thank ye, sur.' And Seamus
   hangs up.

Internet joke

When President Reagan came to Ireland, he was
greeted with a beautifully ambiguous banner which
read 'Welcome to the Ould Sod'.

Dominic Cleary

Seamus says to Sean, 'At me funeral be sure to pour a
   bottle o' whiskey over me grave.'
'Sure,' says Sean, 'but ye wouldn't mind if it was to
   pass through me kidneys first?'

Internet joke

It Isn't This Time of Year at All: Irish Weather

I said, 'It is most extraordinary weather for this time of year.' He replied, 'Ah, it isn't this time of year at all.'

Oliver St John Gogarty, *It Isn't This Time of Year at All* (1954)

Irish weather consists of rain: lots of it. It has been known for the rain to cease, sometimes for as much as two weeks at a time. But when this happens, the Irish complain of drought, pestilence and imminent bankruptcy.

Stan Gebler Davies

You know it is summer in Ireland when the rain gets warmer.

Hal Roach

In a hotel in County Mayo I saw a notice displayed over the barometer: Don't hit me. I am doing my best.

M.F. Watson

The Greatest Talkers: Blarney and Gab

We Irish are too poetical to be poets; we are a nation of brilliant failures, but we are the greatest talkers since the Greeks.

Oscar Wilde, remark to W.B. Yeats, Christmas 1888

If one could only teach the English how to talk and the Irish how to listen, society would be quite civilized.

Oscar Wilde, *An Ideal Husband* (1893)

My one claim to originality among Irishmen is that I never made a speech.

George Moore, *Ave* (1911)

It is often said that in Ireland there is an excess of genius unsustained by talent; but there is talent in the tongues.

V.S. Pritchett, *Midnight Oil* (1971)

If you hear anyone saying 'Begorrah' during your stay in Ireland, you can be sure he's an undercover agent for the Irish Tourist Board pandering to your false expectations.

Terry Eagleton

The Irish equivalent of 'gilding the lily' can be translated as 'rubbing lard on a sow's arse'.

Niall Toibin

Full of Genius, But No Talent

The problem with Ireland is that it's a country full of genius, but with absolutely no talent.

Hugh Leonard, interview in *The Times*, August 1977

It seems to me you do not care what banality a man expresses so long as he expresses it in Irish.

Stephen in James Joyce's *Stephen Hero* (pub. 1944)

Irish Americans:
About as Irish as …

Irish Americans are about as Irish as black Americans are African.

Bob Geldof, quoted in the *Observer*, 22 June 1986

During the potato famine, how come the Irish couldn't afford the cost of a square meal but could still afford to go to America?

Steve Coogan

Every St Patrick's Day every Irishman goes out to find another Irishman to make a speech to.

Shane Leslie, *American Wonderland* (1936)

There are three things I don't like about New York: the water, the buses and the professional Irishmen. A professional Irishman is one who is terribly anxious to pass as a middle-class Englishman.

Brendan Behan, quoted in the *Daily News*, 1961

If you want to bore an Irishman, play him an Irish melody, or introduce him to another Irishman.

George Bernard Shaw, quoted in Michael Holroyd, *Bernard Shaw* (1989)

Now Ireland has her madness and her weather still,
For poetry makes nothing happen.
W.H. Auden, 'In Memory of W.B. Yeats' (1940)

Troglodytic myrmidons; moronic clodhoppers; ignorant bosthoons; poor cawbogues whose only claim to literacy was their blue pencils.
R.M. Smyllie, description of the Irish government censorship department during World War II

All races have produced notable economists, with the exception of the Irish, who doubtless can protest their devotion to the higher arts.
J.K. Galbraith, *The Age of Uncertainty* (1977)

Down with the Whole Damn Lot! Northern Ireland

Down with the bold Sinn Fein!
We'll rout them willy-nilly.
They flaunt their crimes
In the *Belfast Times*,
Which makes *us* look so silly.
Down with the Ulster men!
They don't know which from what.
If Ireland sunk beneath the sea
How peaceful everyone would be!
You haven't said a word about the RUC?
Down with the whole damn lot!
Noël Coward, 'Down with the Whole Damn Lot!', song from *Co-Optimists* (1920s)

For generations, a wide range of shooting in Northern Ireland has provided all sections of the population with a pastime which ... has occupied a great deal of leisure time. Unlike many other countries, the outstanding characteristic of the sport has been that it was not confined to any one class.

Northern Irish Tourist Board, 1969

Anyone who isn't confused here doesn't really understand what's going on.

Anonymous Belfast citizen, 1970

For God's sake, someone bring me a large Scotch. What a bloody awful country.

Reginald Maudling, British Conservative politician, reported comment on a flight back to London, 1 July 1970, after a visit to Northern Ireland in the early years of the Troubles

They say the situation in Northern Ireland is not as bad as they say it is.

Variously attributed to Denis Taylor and an anonymous Irishwoman

The Irish don't know what they want and won't be happy till they get it.

British army officer, 1975

Men have walked on the Sea of Tranquillity, but are still barred from walking through certain parts of Ulster.

Declan Lynch

Beastly Belfast

Belfast ... as uncivilized as ever – savage black mothers in houses of dark red brick, friendly manufacturers too drunk to entertain you when you arrive. It amuses me till I get tired.

E.M. Forster, letter to T.E. Lawrence, 3 May 1928

They should never have shared the Nobel Peace Prize between two people from Northern Ireland. They will only fight over it.

Graham Norton

People who live in this heck's half acre have been worked over by social scientists until there's hardly one of them who's not a footnote on somebody's Master's thesis. And they're so thoroughly journalized that urchins in the street ask, 'Will you be needing a sound bite?' and criticize your choice of shutter speeds.

P.J. O'Rourke, *Holidays in Hell*, 'The Piece of Ireland that Passeth all Understanding' (1988)

North America

The USA: A Giant Mistake

America is a mistake, a giant mistake!
Sigmund Freud

Yankees, Septics and Widow Twankeys

The terms *Yanks* and *Yankees* date from the late 18th century. It has been speculated that *Yankee* comes from the Dutch *Jan Kees* ('John Cheese'), the pejorative name given by Dutch settlers in New Amsterdam (later New York) to the English colonists in Connecticut. Yanks and Yankees have given rise to a range of rhyming slang: *Board and planks* or *Wooden planks*, *Hamshanks*, *Widow Twankeys*, *Shermans* (from the World War II Sherman tanks) and *Septics* (from septic tanks) – hence the Australian version, *Seppos*. A former Chinese nickname for Americans, as noted by William Hickey in Canton in 1809, was *Second Chop Englishmen*.

It was Wonderful to Find America, but ...

It was wonderful to find America, but it would have been more wonderful to miss it.
Mark Twain, *Following the Equator*, 'Conclusion' (1897)

Of course, America had often been discovered before Columbus, but it had always been hushed up.
Oscar Wilde, *Personal Impressions of America* (1883)

Perhaps, after all, America never has been discovered ... I myself would say that it had merely been detected.

Oscar Wilde, *The Picture of Dorian Gray* (1891)

America was discovered accidentally by a great seaman who was looking for something else; when discovered it was not wanted; and most of the exploration for the next fifty years was done in the hope of getting through or round it.

Samuel Eliot Morison, *The Oxford History of the American People* (1965)

When asked by an anthropologist what the Indians called America before the white man came, an Indian said simply, 'Ours.'

Vine Deloria, Jnr

Instead of the Pilgrim Fathers landing on the Plymouth Rock, the Plymouth Rock should have landed on the Pilgrim Fathers.

Anonymous

A Race of Convicts: Brits on the Yanks

In British eyes, it was the rougher sort who left British shores for the colonies – some of them forcibly, to work on the plantations of the Carolinas.

Sir, they are a race of convicts and ought to be grateful for anything we allow them short of hanging.

Samuel Johnson, quoted in James Boswell, *Life of Samuel Johnson* (1791)

According to Oscar

The Americans are certainly hero-worshippers, and always take their heroes from the criminal classes.

Oscar Wilde, letter, 19 April 1882

If one had the money to go to America, one would not go.

Oscar Wilde, quoted in Hesketh Pearson, *The Life of Oscar Wilde* (1946)

MRS ALLONBY: **They say, Lady Hunstanton, that when good Americans die they go to Paris.**
LADY HUNSTANTON: **Indeed? And when bad Americans die, where do they go to?**
LORD ILLINGWORTH: **Oh, they go to America.**

Oscar Wilde, *A Woman of No Importance* (1893)

All Americans lecture, I believe. I suppose it is something in their climate.

Oscar Wilde, *A Woman of No Importance* (1893)

I am willing to love all mankind, *except an American*.

Samuel Johnson, quoted in James Boswell, *Life of Samuel Johnson* (1791). Johnson also described Americans as 'Rascals – Robbers – Pirates'.

Knavery seems to be so much the striking feature of its inhabitants that it may not in the end be an evil that they will become aliens to this country.

George III

Young man, there is America, which at this day serves for little more than to amuse you with stories of savage men and uncouth manners.

Edmund Burke, speech to the House of Commons,
22 March 1775

By the waters of Babylon we sit down and weep, when we think of thee, O America!

Horace Walpole, letter to Mason, 12 June 1775

I do not know the American gentleman, God forgive me for putting two such words together.

Charles Dickens, quoted in Hesketh Pearson, *Dickens* (1949)

Their demeanour is invariably morose, sullen, clownish and repulsive. I should think there is not on the face of the earth a people so entirely destitute of humour, vivacity or the capacity for enjoyment.

Charles Dickens

The Yankee is a dab at electricity and crime,
He tells you how he hustles and it takes him quite a
  time.
I like his hospitality that's cordial and frank,
I do not mind his money but I do not like his swank.

G.K. Chesterton, 'A Song of Self-esteem', in *Collected Poems* (1933)

I don't believe they have any God and their hats are frightful. On balance I prefer the Arabs.

Freya Stark, letter, 19 February 1944

Lunatics and Idiots: GBS on the US of A

An asylum for the sane would be empty in America.

The 100% American is 99% idiot.

You are right in your impression that a number of persons are urging me to come to the United States. But why on earth do you call them my friends?

Americans adore me and will go on adoring me until I say something nice about them.

George Bernard Shaw

When millions of GIs were 'over-paid, over-sexed and over here' during World War II, one English journalist gave this advice to his readers:

In fairness to our guests, we should remember these few but fundamental facts:

That they are foreigners. Only a small percentage have any British forebears. ...

That though we may be spiritually far more civilized, materially they have the advantage ...

That like all children they are very sensitive. They

mistake our British reticence and reserve for the cold
shoulder and positive dislike.

S.P.B. Mais, in the *Bristol Evening Post*, 29 February 1944

We are all American at puberty: we die French.

Evelyn Waugh, *Diaries*, 18 July 1961

**Americans have plenty of everything and the best of
nothing.**

John Keats, *You Might As Well Live* (1970)

Of the USA:
I have seen the future and it does not work.

Philip Toynbee, in the *Observer*, 27 January 1974

Too Nice for Their Own Good ...

**They don't stand on ceremony ... they make no
distinction about a man's background, his parentage,
his education. They say what they mean, and there is a
vivid muscularity about the way they say it ... They are
always the first to put their hands in their pockets.
They press you to visit them in their own home the
moment they meet you, and are irrepressibly good-
humoured, ambitious and brimming with self-
confidence in any company. Apart from all that I've got
nothing against them.**

Tom Stoppard, *Dirty Linen* (1976), spoken by a British civil
servant

In England you have to know people very intimately indeed before they tell you about the rust in their Volvo. It has never surprised me that there are fifty million Roman Catholics in America, and nearly as many psychiatrists: bean-spilling is the national mania.

Alan Coren, reviewing Kurt Vonnegut's *Palm Sunday* in the *Sunday Times*, 21 June 1981

A Nazi Speaks

The Americans cannot build aeroplanes. They are very good at refrigerators and razor blades.

Hermann Goering, remark to Adolf Hitler, December 1940

I *do* detest the Americans. They expect everyone to go to the devil at the same hectic pace as themselves. It takes hundreds of years to do it properly. Look at us.

John le Carré, *The Tailor of Panama* (1996)

I Tremble for My Country: Yanks on the Yanks

I tremble for my country when I reflect that God is just.

Thomas Jefferson, *Notes on the State of Virginia* (1784–5)

In America the geography is sublime, but the men are not.

Ralph Waldo Emerson, *The Conduct of Life*, 'Considerations by the Way' (1860)

The Malevolence of Mencken

H.L. Mencken, the US journalist and critic, reserved much of his bile for his fellow countrymen:

The American people, taking one with another, constitute the most timorous, snivelling, poltroonish, ignominious mob of serfs and goose-steppers ever gathered under one flag in Christendom since the end of the Middle Ages.

H.L. Mencken, *Prejudices: Third Series* (1922)

q: **If you find so much that is unworthy of reverence in the United States, why do you live here?**
a: **Why do men go to zoos?**

H.L. Mencken, *Prejudices: Fifth Series* (1926)

No one in this world, so far as I know – and I have searched the records for years, and employed agents to help me – has ever lost money by underestimating the intelligence of the great masses of the plain people. Nor has anyone ever lost public office thereby.

H.L. Mencken, in the *Chicago Tribune*, 19 September 1926

I see America as a black curse upon the world.

Henry Miller, *Black Spring* (1936)

We don't know what we want, but we are ready to bite somebody to get it.

Will Rogers

California: The Department-Store State

California is a great place – if you happen to be an orange.

Fred Allen, in *American Magazine*, December 1945

It's a scientific fact that if you live in California you lose one point of your IQ every year.

Truman Capote

In California, handicapped parking is for women who are frigid.

Joan Rivers

America is a nation that conceives many odd inventions for getting somewhere but can think of nothing to do when it gets there.

Will Rogers

I have never been able to look upon America as young and vital, but rather as prematurely old, as a fruit which rotted before it had a chance to ripen.

Henry Miller, *The Air-Conditioned Nightmare* (1945)

America is the only place where you buy a lifetime supply of aspirin for one dollar, and use it up in two weeks.

John Barrymore

In the United States, there one feels free ... Except from Americans – but every pearl has its oyster.
Randall Jarrell, *Pictures from an Institution* (1954)

Los Angeles: Nineteen Suburbs in Search of a Metropolis
H.L. Mencken, *Americana* (1925)

A big hard-boiled city with no more personality than a paper cup.
Raymond Chandler, *The Little Sister* (1949)

The reason there's so much smog in LA is so God can't see what they're doing down there.
Glen Campbell, quoted in Maxim Jabukowski (ed.), *The Wit and Wisdom of Rock and Roll* (1983)

The difference between Los Angeles and yoghurt is that yoghurt has real culture.
Tom Taussik, *Legless in Gaza*. The same has been said of Australia.

It's like paradise, with a lobotomy.
Jane Fonda speaking in Neil Simon's film *California Suite* (1978)

There are two million interesting people in New York and only seventy-eight in Los Angeles.
Neil Simon, interview in *Playboy*, February 1979

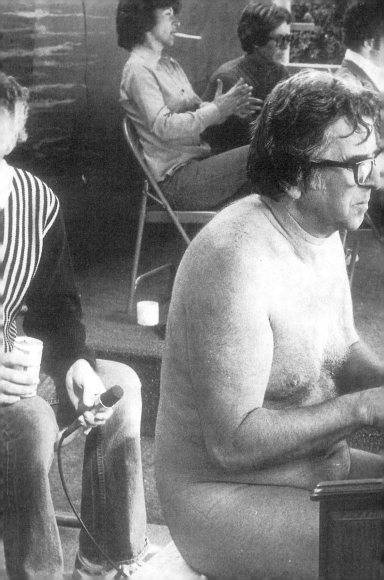

America is not a young land: it is old and dirty and evil before the settlers, before the Indians. The evil is there waiting.

William Burroughs, *The Naked Lunch* (1959)

Chicago: Hog Butcher for the World

Here is the difference between Dante, Milton, and me. They wrote about hell and never saw the place. I wrote about Chicago after looking the town over for years and years.

Carl Sandburg, quoted in Harry Golden, *Carl Sandburg* (1961)

It is a joint where the bulls and the foxes live well and the lambs wind up head-down from the hook.

Nelson Algren, *Chicago: City on the Make* (1951)

The trouble with America is that there are far too many wide open spaces surrounded by teeth.

Charles Luckman

America is the ultimate denial of the theory of man's continuous evolution.

H. Rap Brown, *Die Nigger Die!* (1969)

WE A badddDDD PEOPLE

Sonia Sanchez, title of a 1973 poetry collection

Violence Punctuated by Committee Meetings: American Football

Football combines the two worst things about America: it is violence punctuated by committee meetings.

George F. Will, quoted in the *International Herald Tribune*, 1990

College football today is one of the last great strongholds of genuine old-fashioned American hypocrisy.

Paul Gallico, *Farewell to Sport* (1938)

Kicking is very important in football. In fact, some of the more enthusiastic players even kick the ball, occasionally.

Alfred Hitchcock

To see some of our best-educated boys spending the afternoon knocking each other down, while thousands cheer them on, hardly gives a picture of a peace-loving nation.

Lyndon Baines Johnson, quoted in the *New York Times*, 1967

Rugby is a beastly game played by gentlemen. Soccer is a gentleman's game played by beasts. Football is a beastly game played by beasts.

Henry Blaha, in 1972

Football is the only game you come into with a semblance of intelligence and end up a babbling moron.

Mike Adamie, American football player

That Yaptown on the Hudson called New York

**If there ever was an aviary overstocked with jays it is
that Yaptown on the Hudson called New York.**
O. Henry, *Gentle Grafter*, 'A Tempered Wind' (1908)

**A car is useless in New York, essential everywhere else.
The same with good manners.**
Mignon McLaughlin, *The Second Neurotic's Notebook* (1966)

**New York is the only city in the world where you can get
deliberately run over on the sidewalk by a pedestrian.**
Russell Baker

**New York now leads the world's great cities in the
number of people around whom you shouldn't make a
sudden move.**
David Letterman, *Late Night with David Letterman*,
9 February 1984

**I've come to think of Europe as a hardcover book,
America as the paperback version.**
Owen Brademas, in Don DeLillo, *The Names* (1982)

**Americans would rather live next to a pervert heroin
addict Communist pornographer than a person with an
unkempt lawn.**
Dave Barry, *The Taming of the Screw* (1983)

I've been a New Yorker for ten years, and the only people who are nice to us turn out to be Moonies.

P.J. O'Rourke, in *Rolling Stone*, 1982

New York is an exciting town where something is happening all the time, most of it unsolved.

Johnny Carson

Manhattan:
A narrow island off the coast of New Jersey devoted to the pursuit of lunch.

Raymond Sokolov, in the *Wall Street Journal*, 1984

The Bronx?
No thonx!

Ogden Nash, 'Geographical Reflection', in the *New Yorker*, 1931

In the midst of life we are in Brooklyn.

Oliver Herford

One Long Expectoration: American Manners

America is one long expectoration.

Oscar Wilde

European visitors to America in the 19th century were struck by the sheer quantity of hawking and spitting, together with the absence of other niceties.

The total want of the usual courtesies of the table, the voracious rapidity with which the viands were seized and devoured; the strange uncouth phrases and pronunciation; the loathsome spitting, from the contamination of which it was absolutely impossible to protect our dresses; the frightful manner of feeding

The Beaten, Ignorant, Bible-Ridden, White South
Sherwood Anderson (1876–1941)

Storytelling and copulation are the two chief forms of amusement in the South. They're inexpensive and easy to procure.
Robert Penn Warren, quoted in *Newsweek*, 25 August 1980

The average Southerner has the speech patterns of someone slipping in and out of consciousness. I can change my shoes and socks faster than most people in Mississippi can speak a sentence.
Bill Bryson, *The Lost Continent* (1989)

I happen to know quite a bit about the South. Spent twenty years there one night.
Dick Gregory

with their knives, till the whole blade seemed to enter into the mouth, and the still more frightful manner of cleaning the teeth afterwards with a pocket-knife, soon forced us to feel that ... the dinner-hour was to be anything rather than an hour of enjoyment.

Frances Trollope (1780–1863)

You can never conceive what the hawking and spitting is the whole night through. Last night was the worst. Upon my honour and word, I was obliged, this morning, to lay my fur coat on the deck and wipe the half-dried flakes of spittle from it with my handkerchief. The only surprise seemed to be that I should consider it necessary to do so ...

Charles Dickens

The American characteristic is Uncourteousness. We are the impolite Nation ... It is only in uncourteousness, incivility, impoliteness, that we stand alone – until hell shall be heard from.

Mark Twain, *Mark Twain's Notebook* (ed. A.B. Paine, 1935)

When it comes down to pure ornamental cursing, the native American is gifted above the sons of man.

Mark Twain, *Roughing It* (1872)

It is absurd to say that there are neither ruins nor curiosities in America when they have their mothers and their manners.

Oscar Wilde

America is the only nation in history which miraculously has gone directly from barbarism to degeneration without the usual interval of civilization.
Georges Clemenceau

A Chaos of Ugliness: American Culture

'A chaos of ugliness' was the artist Edward Hopper's description of the USA.

This will never be a civilized country until we spend more money for books than we do for chewing gum.
Elbert Hubbard (1856–1915), US editor and writer

There at any rate is a country that has no trappings, no pageantry, and no gorgeous ceremonies. I saw only two processions – one was the Fire Brigade preceded by the Police, the other was the Police preceded by the Fire Brigade.
Oscar Wilde, *Impressions of America* (pub. 1906)

The American artist ...
The unwanted cockroach in the kitchen of a frontier society.
John Sloan (1871–1951), American painter, quoted in Barbara Rose, *American Art since 1900* (1967)

What a horror it is for a whole nation to be developing without the sense of beauty, and eating bananas for breakfast.
Edith Wharton, letter to Sara Norton, 19 August 1904

American music ... today has no class whatsoever and is mere barbaric mouthing.

Jerome Kern, quoted in the *New York Times*, 1920

All the arts in America are a gigantic racket run by unscrupulous men for unhealthy women.

Sir Thomas Beecham

In other countries, art and literature are left to a lot of shabby bums living in attics and feeding on booze and spaghetti, but in America the successful writer or picture-painter is indistinguishable from any other decent business man.

Sinclair Lewis, *Babbitt* (1922)

The trouble with us in America isn't that the poetry of life has turned to prose, but that it has turned to advertising copy.

Louis Kronenberger, *Company Manners*, 'The Spirit of the Age' (1954)

Americans may have no identity, but they do have wonderful teeth.

Jean Baudrillard, *America* (1986)

Oh, oh, irony! Oh, no, no. We don't get that here. See, uh, people ski topless here while smoking dope, so irony's not really a high priority. We haven't had any irony here since about '83, when I was the only practitioner of it, and I stopped because I was tired of being stared at.

Steve Martin speaking his own lines in the film *Roxanne* (1987)

Divided by a Common Language

England and America are two countries divided only by a common language.

George Bernard Shaw, attributed remark

We have really everything in common with America nowadays, except, of course, language.

Oscar Wilde, 'The Canterville Ghost' (1887)

The American has no language. He has dialect, slang, provincialism, accent and so forth.

Rudyard Kipling

When the American people get through with the English language, it will look as if it had been run over by a musical comedy.

Finley Peter Dunne, *Mr Dooley at His Best* (1938)

To an American actor recently back from Britain, who pronounced 'schedule' in the British way:
If you don't mind my saying so, I think you're full of skit.

Dorothy Parker

Westward Ho!

These people are simple farmers, people of the land, the common clay of the New West. You know – morons.

Mel Brooks, screenplay for *Blazing Saddles* (1974)

Only One Sauce: American Cuisine

I found there a country with thirty-two religions and only one sauce.

Charles-Maurice de Talleyrand. Talleyrand was in exile in America, 1794–6.

I would rather live in Russia on black bread and vodka than in the United States at the best hotels. America knows nothing of food, love, or art.

Isadora Duncan, interview, 1922

The national dish of America is menus.

Robert Robinson, British broadcaster

To barbecue is a way of life rather than a desirable method of cooking.

Clement Freud, *Freud on Food* (1978)

If you're going to America, bring your own food.

Fran Lebowitz, *Social Studies* (1981)

If figures of speech based on sports and fornication were suddenly banned, American corporate communication would be reduced to pure mathematics.

Jay McInerney, *Brightness Falls* (1992)

Guys, Dolls and Serial Polygamy

The Americans, like the English, probably make love worse than any other race.

Walt Whitman

American women expect to find in their husbands a perfection that English women only hope to find in their butlers.

W. Somerset Maugham, *A Writer's Notebook* (1949)

Marriage is hardly a thing one can do now and then – except in America.

Oscar Wilde

France may claim the happiest marriages in the world, but the happiest divorces in the world are 'made in America'.

Helen Rowland, *A Guide to Men*, 'What Every Woman Wonders' (1922)

Overheard by Rula Lenska at a Hollywood wedding reception:
Q: **'What are you giving the bride and groom?'**
A: **'Oh, about three months.'**

[Americans are] better at having a love affair that lasts ten minutes than any other people in the world.

Stephen Spender, interview in the *New York Post*, 1975

There's a sexual revolution going on, and I think that with our current foreign policy, we'll probably be sending troops in there any minute to break it up.

Mel Brooks

American men:
I never saw an American man walk or stand well – they are nearly all hollow chested and round shouldered.

Frances Trollope (1780–1863)

All American writing gives me the impression that Americans don't care for girls at all. What the American male really wants is two things: he wants to be blown by a stranger while reading the newspaper, and he wants to be fucked by his buddy when he's drunk.

W.H. Auden

The American male does not mature until he has exhausted all other possibilities.

Wilfred Sheed

All American males are failed athletes.

Pete Gent, in the *Weekend Guardian*, 8–9 July 1989

American women:

You can never be too rich or too thin.

Duchess of Windsor (Mrs Wallis Simpson)

Washington – Hubbub of the Universe

Anonymous, in *Reader's Digest*

Washington is a city of southern efficiency and northern charm.

John F. Kennedy, remark, 1962

People only leave by way of the box – ballot or coffin.

Claiborne Pell, in *Vogue*, 1 August 1963

Washington DC is a little too small to be a state, but too large to be an asylum for the mentally deranged.

Anne Burford, speech, 1984

America is the only country in the world where a housewife hires a woman to do her cleaning so she can do volunteer work at the day-care centre where the cleaning woman leaves her child.

Milton Berle

JOURNALIST: **Why have you come to America, Mr Thomas?**
DYLAN THOMAS: **In pursuit of my life-long quest for naked women in wet mackintoshes.**

Quoted in Constantine Fitzgibbon, *Dylan Thomas* (1965)

Thou Boasted Land of Liberty ...

**America it is to thee, Thou boasted land of liberty,
– It is to thee I raise my song,
Thou land of blood, and crime, and wrong.**

James M. Whitfield (1830–70), 'America'

America is where the wildest humans on the planet came to do anything they damn pleased.

P.J. O'Rourke, in *Rolling Stone*, 1982

Give me your tired, your poor, your huddled masses yearning to be free, provided they have satisfactorily filled out forms 3584-A through 3597-Q.

Dwight McDonald

It is by the goodness of God that in our country we have those three unspeakably precious things: freedom of speech, freedom of conscience, and the prudence never to practise either of them.

Mark Twain

You hear about constitutional rights, free speech and the free press. Every time I hear these words I say to myself, 'That man is a Red, that man is a Communist!' You never hear a real American talk like that.

Frank Hague, Democratic 'boss' of Jersey City and Hudson county, 1917–47

America is a land where a citizen will cross the ocean to fight for democracy – and won't cross the street to vote in a national election.

Bill Vaughan

Is the US ready for self-government?

Graffito, New York, 1971

A Nation Ruled by Swine

In a nation ruled by swine, all pigs are upwardly mobile – and the rest of us are fucked ...

Hunter S. Thompson, 'Jacket Copy for *Fear and Loathing in Las Vegas*', in *The Great Shark Hunt* (1979)

Texas vs. Hell

If I owned Texas and hell, I would rent out Texas and live in hell.

Philip Henry Sheridan (1831–88), US general, remark in officers' mess, Fort Clark, Texas, 1855

Un-American Activities

'There won't be any revolution in America,' said
Isadore. Nikitin agreed. 'The people are too clean.
They spend all their time changing their shirts
and washing themselves. You can't feel fierce and
revolutionary in a bathroom.'
Eric Linklater, *Juan in America* (1931)

American's dissidents are not committed to
mental hospitals and sent into exile; they thrive
and prosper and buy a house in Nantucket and
take flyers in the commodities market.
Ted Morgan, *On Becoming American* (1978)

Leading one to conclude that:
It is a country equally divided between
conservatives and reactionaries.
Gore Vidal, interview in the *Observer*, 16 September 1984

America is still a government of the naïve, for the
naïve, and by the naïve.
Christopher Morley, *Inward Ho!* (1923)

In England, the system is benign and the people are
hostile. In America, the people are friendly – and the
system is brutal!
Quentin Crisp, interviewed in the *Guardian*, 23 October 1985

The American political system is like fast food – mushy, insipid, made out of disgusting parts of things and everybody wants some.

P.J. O'Rourke, *Parliament of Whores* (1991)

Brain-dead in Boston

I guess God made Boston on a wet Sunday.

Raymond Chandler, letter to Bernice Baumgarten, 21 March 1949

I have just returned from Boston. It is the only thing to do if you find yourself up there.

Fred Allen, letter to Groucho Marx, 1953

At the top of it all is the President:

When I was a boy I was told that anybody could become President; I'm beginning to believe it.

Clarence Darrow, quoted in Irving Stone, *Clarence Darrow for the Defence* (1941)

In America any boy may become President, and I suppose that's just the risk he takes.

Adlai Stevenson, in 1952

Then there's Congress:

Reader, suppose you were an idiot. And suppose you were a member of Congress. But I repeat myself.

Mark Twain, quoted in A.B. Paine, *Mark Twain: A Biography* (1912)

The organization of American society is an interlocking system of semi-monopolies notoriously venal, an electorate notoriously unenlightened, misled by mass media notoriously phoney.

Paul Goodman, *The Community of Scholars* (1962)

We have a long way to go in meeting the standards of most democracies on earth.

Jimmy Carter, former US president, quoted in the *Observer*, 1 April 2001

Hey, Hey, It's the American Way!

The true religion of America has always been America.

Norman Mailer, interviewed in *Time Out*, 1984

Violence is as American as cherry pie.

H. Rap Brown, *Die Nigger Die!* (1969)

America is the child society par excellence ... a society of all rights and no obligations ... the only society that ever raised gangsterism to the status of myth, and murder to the status of tragedy or politics.

Karl Shapiro, 'To Abolish Children', in *To Abolish Children and Other Essays* (1968)

America is a vast conspiracy to make you happy.

John Updike, 'How to Love America and Leave It at the Same Time', in *Problems* (1980)

From Dream to Nightmare …

One step up the Transcendental Ladder from the American Way
squats the American Dream …

**HUSBAND (*TO WIFE*): The egg timer is pinging. The toaster is
popping. The coffeepot is perking. Is this it, Alice? Is
this the great American dream?**
Henry Martin, cartoon in the *New Yorker*

**The American dream turned belly up, turned green,
bobbed to the scummy surface of cupidity unlimited,
filled with gas, went *bang* in the noonday sun.**
Kurt Vonnegut, *God Bless You, Mr Rosewater* (1965)

**America is a country that doesn't know where it
is going but is determined to set a speed record
getting there.**
Laurence J. Peter, *Quotations for Our Time* (1977)

**… the American Dream, according to which everybody
thinks they can get rich quick, and if they can't do it by
legal means then they'll do it by illegal ones.**
Martin Scorsese, discussing his film *Mean Streets*, in *Scorsese
on Scorsese* (1989)

The Rear End of an Ostrich

**Every time Europe looks across the Atlantic to see
the American eagle, it observes only the rear end
of an ostrich.**
H.G. Wells

The United States has much to offer the Third World War.
Ronald Reagan, speech, 1975

Reagan's successor's vice-president showed a similar grasp of foreign affairs:
The Holocaust was an obscene period in our nation's history – no, not in our nation's history but in World War Two. I mean in this century's history. But we all lived in this century. I didn't live in this century, but in this century's history.
James Danforth Quayle, speech, 15 September 1988

Americans can share the English belief that God is anglophone:
Imagine the Lord speaking French! Aside from a few words in Hebrew, I took it completely for granted that God had never spoken anything but the most dignified English.
Clarence Day

Being Fools Overseas: Americans Abroad

So everyone's a fool outside their own country. America, having emerged from World War II as the only country with any money left, got a twenty-year head start on being fools overseas.
P.J. O'Rourke, interviewed in the *Observer*, 15 January 1989

That strange blend of the commercial traveller, the missionary, and the barbarian conqueror, which was the American abroad.
Olaf Stapleton, *Last and First Men* (1931)

American GIs in Britain during World War II:

Overpaid, overfed, oversexed, and over here.

Possibly coined by the English comedian Tommy Trinder

A group of innocent American tourists was taken on a tour bus through a country the members later described as 'either France or Sweden', and subjected to three days of looking at old dirty buildings where it was not possible to get a cheeseburger.

Dave Barry

Americans get nervous abroad. As a result they tend either to travel in groups or bomb Libya.

Miles Kington, in the *Independent*, 29 March 1989

Any Idiot Can Play It: Baseball

Baseball is the favorite American sport because it's so slow. Any idiot can follow it. And just about any idiot can play it.

Gore Vidal

Two hours is as long as an American will wait for the close of a baseball game – or anything for that matter.

Albert G. Spalding, US baseball manufacturer

I don't think I can be expected to take seriously any game which takes less than three days to reach its conclusion.

Tom Stoppard, quoted in the *Guardian*, 24 December 1984

If You Piss Us Off We'll Bomb Your Cities

We're Americans, we're a simple people, but if you piss us off we'll bomb your cities.
Robin Williams

God protects fools, drunks and the United States of America.
Otto von Bismarck

Instead of leading the world, America appears to have resolved to buy it.
Thomas Mann, letter, 1947

America is a large, friendly dog in a very small room. Every time it wags its tail it knocks over a chair.
Arnold Toynbee, remark, 1954

Frustrate a Frenchman, he will drink himself to death; an Irishman, he will die of angry hypertension; a Dane, he will shoot himself; an American, he will get drunk, shoot you, then establish a million-dollar aid programme for your relatives. Then he will die of an ulcer.
Stanley Rudin, in the *New York Times*, 1963

America ... just a nation of two hundred million used car salesmen with all the money we need to buy guns and no qualms about killing anybody else in the world who tries to make us uncomfortable.
Hunter S. Thompson, *Fear and Loathing on the Campaign Trail* (1972)

The Great Satan.
Ayatollah Ruhollah Khomeini (1908–89), describing the USA

Extremely Boring Canada

Racial characteristics: hard to tell a Canadian from an extremely boring regular white person unless he's dressed to go outdoors. Very little is known of the Canadian country since it is rarely visited by anyone but the Queen and illiterate sport fishermen.

P.J. O'Rourke, 'Foreigners Around the World', in *National Lampoon*, 1976

The beginning of Canadian cultural nationalism was not 'Am I really that oppressed?' but 'Am I really that boring?'

Margaret Atwood, Canadian novelist, interview in the *Ontario Review*, 1978

Canadians represent, as it were, the least militant North American minority group. The white, Protestant, heterosexual ghetto of the north.

Mordecai Richler, Canadian humorist

Newfoundland: Dogs, Hogs and Fogs

I find that Newfoundland is said to be celebrated for its codfish, its dogs, its hogs, its fogs.

Sir William Whiteway (1828–1908)

A Canadian is someone who knows how to make love in a canoe.
Pierre Berton

The cold narrow minds, the confined ideals, the by-gone prejudices of the society are hardly conceivable; books there are none, nor music, and as to pictures! the Lord deliver us from such! The people do not know what a picture is.
Anna Jameson (1794–1860), Canadian writer

How utterly destitute of all light and charm are the intellectual conditions of our people and the institutions of our public life! How barren! How barbarous!
Archibald Lampman (1861–99), Canadian poet

Prince Edward Island: A Lump of Worthlessness

The explanation of why the people of Prince Edward Island are called *Spud Islanders* is to be found in the following observation:

A rascally heap of sand, rock and swamp, called Prince Edward Island, in the horrible Gulf of St Lawrence; that lump of worthlessness bears nothing but potatoes.

William Cobbett, who as a young man was with the army in Canada, returning to England in 1791

Canada is a country without a soul – live, but, unlike the States, not kicking.
Rupert Brooke, who spent 1913–14 wandering in the USA, Canada and the South Pacific. He also remarked: 'The only poet in Canada was very nice to me in Ottawa. Canada's a bloody place for a sensitive real poet like this to live all his life in.'

Eskimos

An Eskimo has a broken snowmobile, so he brings it in to be serviced. After checking it out, the mechanic says, 'Looks like you blew a seal.'
　　The Eskimo looks at him and says, 'No, that's just frost on my moustache.'
Internet joke

You have to know a man awfully well in Canada to know his surname.
John Buchan, the British novelist, who as Lord Tweedsmuir was appointed governor general of Canada in 1935; quoted in the *Observer*, 1950

Canada is a country where nothing seems ever to happen. A country always dressed in its Sunday go-to-meeting clothes. A country you wouldn't ask to dance a second waltz. Clean. Christian. Dull. Quiescent.
Carol Shields, *The Stone Diaries* (1993). Shields is not only a novelist, but also chancellor of the University of Winnipeg.

Canada is not really a place where you are encouraged to have large spiritual adventures.
Robertson Davies, *The Enthusiasms of Robertson Davies*, 'The Table Talk of Robertson Davies' (1990). Davies was master of Massey College, University of Toronto, as well as a novelist.

Canada is a country so square that even the female impersonators are women.
Line from the Canadian film *Outrageous!* (1977)

My generation of Canadians grew up believing that, if we were very good or very smart, or both, we would someday graduate from Canada.
Robert Fulford

'I'm world-famous,' Dr Parks said, 'all over Canada.'
Mordecai Richler, *The Incomparable Auk* (1963)

My theory is that if you can make it in Canada, you can make it anywhere.
Bernard Slade

Outside the Stream of History

This gloomy region, where the year is divided into one day and one night, lies entirely outside the stream of history.
W.W. Reade (1814–84)

Canada's climate is nine months winter and three months late in the fall.
Evan Esar

Canada is only useful to provide me with furs.
Mme de Pompadour, after the fall of Quebec in 1759

Canada's history is as dull as ditchwater and her politics is full of it.
Maurice Hutton, in *The Canadian Historical Review*, 1936

Fellow citizens, this country is going to the dogs hand over hand.
T.C. Haliburton (1796–1865), Canadian writer

Canada is a secondary and second-rate country without much depth of experience: everyone admits that – too freely.
A.R.M. Lower, in *The Canadian Historical Review*, 1941

Toronto: A House of Ill Fame

Houses of ill fame in Toronto? Certainly not. The whole city is an immense house of ill fame.
C.S. Clark (1826–1909)

Toronto as a city carries out the idea of Canada as a country. It is a calculated crime both against the aspirations of the human soul and the affection of the heart.
Aleister Crowley

Toronto will be a fine town, when it's finished.
Brendan Behan

In Pierre Elliott Trudeau, Canada has at last produced a political leader worthy of assassination.

Irving Layton, *The Whole Bloody Bird*, 'Obo II' (1969)

Canadians do not like heroes, and so they do not have them.

George Woodcock, *Canada and the Canadians* (1970)

British Columbia: Bad to Worse

British Columbia is a barren, cold mountain country that is not worth keeping. The place has been going from bad to worse.

Henry Labouchère (1798–1869)

In Canada we don't ban demonstrations, we re-route them.

Alan Borovoy

The beaver is a good national symbol for Canada. He's so busy chewing he can't see what's going on.

Howard Cable

The Vichyssoise of Nations

In any world menu, Canada must be considered the vichyssoise of nations – it's cold, half-French, and difficult to stir.

Stuart Keate

In the 18th century the British and French fought over possession of Canada:

You know that these two nations are at war for a few acres of snow, and that they are spending more than all Canada is worth.

Voltaire

Canada could have enjoyed:
English government,
French culture,
And American know-how.
Instead it ended up with:
English know-how,
French government,
And American culture.

John Robert Colombo, 'O Canada', in *The New Romans* (1968, ed. Al Purdy)

Canada has never been a melting pot; more like a tossed salad.

Arnold Edinborough

Canada is a collection of ten provinces with strong governments loosely connected by fear.

Dave Broadfoot

Nova Scotia: Good God

Good God, what sums the nursing of that ill-troven, hard-visaged and ill-favoured brat, Nova Scotia, has cost this nation.

Edmund Burke

Canada has no cultural unity, no linguistic unity, no religious unity, no economic unity, no geographic unity. All it has is unity.
Kenneth Boulding

Canada is the only country in the world that knows how to live without an identity.
Marshall McLuhan

Upper and Lower

French Canada is a relic of the historical past preserved by isolation, as Siberian mammoths are preserved by ice.
Goldwin Smith, *The Political Destiny of Canada* (1878)

Gentlemen, I give you Upper Canada; because I don't want it myself.
Artemus Ward (1834–67), US humorist. Upper Canada approximates to modern Ontario.

If the national mental illness of the United States is megalomania, that of Canada is paranoid schizophrenia.
Margaret Atwood

America's Attic

Canada is America's attic.
Robertson Davies

Canada is a by-product of the United States.

Archibald MacMechan, in *The Canadian Historical Review*, 1920

I fear that I have not got much to say about Canada, not having seen much; what I got by going to Canada was a cold.

Henry David Thoreau (1817–62), US writer

I don't even know what street Canada is on.

Al Capone, in 1931

When they said Canada, I thought it would be up in the mountains somewhere.

Marilyn Monroe

We tended to imagine Canada as a vast hunting preserve convenient to the United States.

Edmund Wilson, *O Canada: An American's Notes on Canadian Culture* (1965)

Americans are benevolently ignorant about Canada, while Canadians are malevolently well informed about the United States.

J. Bartlet Brebner

Canadians are concerned about the rape of our country by the Americans. And I say that it is not true – how can you rape a prostitute?

Dave Broadfoot

Canada helps make our napalm and then takes in our deserters. Canada has both ends of a dirty stick and ends up with both hands dirty.

Daniel Berrigan

Everywhere Else

Latin America: All Individual Countries

Well, I learned a lot. … You'd be surprised. They're all individual countries.

Ronald Reagan, returning from a tour of South America in 1982

While on tour, Reagan was still trying to sort them out …

Now would you join me in a toast to President Figueredo, to the people of Bolivia – no, that's where I'm going – to the people of Brazil.

Speech during a visit to Colombia, 1982

I'd never heard of this place Guatemala until I was in my seventy-ninth year.

Winston Churchill, remark in June 1954 while visiting the USA

You must not judge people by their country. In South America, it is always wise to judge people by their altitude.

Paul Theroux, quoting an old lady, in *The Old Patagonian Express* (1979)

Bolivians are merely metamorphosed llamas who have learned to talk but not think.

José Toribio Merino, Bolivian writer

Poor Mexico! So far from God, so close to the United States.

Porfirio Diaz (1830-1915), president of Mexico

The United States looks upon Mexico as a good neighbour, a strong upholder of democratic traditions in this hemisphere, and a country we are proud to call our own.

Edward Stettinius, US secretary of state, on an official visit to Mexico in February 1945. His officials had a job putting that one right.

Mexico is an arch-transvestite, a tragic buffoon. … Mother Mexico doesn't even bother to shave her mustachios.

Richard Rodriguez, *Frontiers*, 'Night and Day' (1990)

A Pimple on the Ass of Progress

The Anglo-Argentinian conflict over the Falkland Islands:
This has been a pimple on the ass of progress festering for 200 years, and I guess someone decided to lance it.

Alexander Haig, then US secretary of state, quoted in the *Sunday Times*, 1982

The Falklands thing was a fight between two bald men over a comb.

Jorge Luis Borges, in *Time*, 14 February 1983

GOTCHA!

Sun headline, 4 May 1982, on the sinking of the Argentinian cruiser *General Belgrano* by a British submarine

Incidentally, British soldiers posted to the Falklands refer to the islanders as *Bennies*, after the rather dim rustic character in the TV soap opera *Crossroads*.

Africa:
The Dark Incontinent

The late Alan Clark, government minister and roving he-goat of the Conservative Party, notoriously referred to Africa as **Bongo-Bongo Land.**

Many others have been equally ignorant and/or dismissive:

The Caffres, at the Cape of Good Hope, piss upon those whom they delight to honour.
Tobias Smollett, *Travels through France and Italy* (1766)

The African is my brother – but he is my younger brother by several centuries.
Albert Schweitzer, French missionary, in 1955

Every time I see a picture of those people in Somalia it brings a tear to my eye. I mean I'd love to be that thin but not with all those flies and everything.
Mariah Carey, US pop singer

If we had spent £167 million on condoms we wouldn't have had these problems in the first place.
Nicholas Fairbairn, Conservative MP, on emergency food aid to Africa, 12 May 1991

When asked for a comment on South Africa during the apartheid era, the soap and pop star Kylie Minogue, was baffled:
Er ... they shouldn't be killing the rhinos.

President Sese Seko Mobuto of Zaire (now the Democratic Republic of Congo) sought to defend the honour of his countrymen in 1978:

The people of Zaire are not thieves. It merely happens that they take more things, or borrow them.

Why the hell do I want to go to a place like Mombasa? ... I just see myself in a pot of boiling water with all these natives dancing around me.

Mel Lastman, mayor of Toronto, prior to a trip to Africa to promote his city's bid to host the 2008 Olympics, quoted in the *Guardian*, 30 June 2001

Diarrhoea City

Particular places in Africa have come in for abomination of one kind or another:

'Diarrhoea City', oh fuck yes, terrible place. You don't even have to eat anything for that. It's the dust from the camel shit. One of the worst places I've ever been.

Michael Caine, referring to Ouarzazate, Morocco

Addis Ababa looks as if it has been dragged piecemeal from an aeroplane carrying rubbish.

John Gunther

Some places in Africa have been found depressing for different reasons. Here is Alan Coren on what was then Rhodesia (now Zimbabwe):

It is a suburb pretending to be a country.

Boers and Brutes: South Africa

South Africa, renowned both far and wide
For politics and little else beside.
Roy Campbell, 'The Wayzgoose' (1928)

Apartheid-era South Africa came in for condemnation from
around the world – and from South Africans themselves:

Christ in this country would quite likely have been
arrested under the Suppression of Communism Act.
Joost de Blank, archbishop of Cape Town, in 1963

South Africa is developing a nubitron. The nuclear
device, still in its earliest stages of development,
would destroy non-whites, while leaving property and
Caucasians unharmed. The nubitron would be used for
peaceful purposes, diplomats said in Pretoria.
Off the Wall Street Journal, 1982

How many South African policemen does it take to
break an egg?
None. It fell down the stairs.
Anonymous

For decades the Afrikaners doggedly resisted change:
There is only one element that can break the Afrikaner,
and that is the Afrikaner himself. It is when the
Afrikaner, like a baboon shot in the stomach, pulls out
his own intestines. We must guard against that.
P.W. Botha, South African prime minister, speech, 26 April 1984

The Middle East:
Trouble in Shovelfuls

I come from a land, from a faraway place
Where the caravan camels roam.
Where they cut off your ear if they don't like your face.
It's barbaric, but – hey – it's home.
Howard Ashman and Alan Menken, song from the Disney
cartoon *Aladdin* (1992). In the British release of the film the
third line was changed to 'Where it's flat and immense and the
heat is intense.'

The Arabs are only Jews upon horseback.
Benjamin Disraeli, *Tancred* (1847)

I do not seek for camel's milk nor the sight of an Arab.
Turkish saying

The price of oil is not determined by the British
Parliament. It is determined by some lads riding
camels who do not even know how to spell 'national
sovereignty'.
Vic Feather, former general secretary of the TUC, 1975

They should settle this problem in a true Christian
spirit.
Warren Austin, US delegate to the UN, on the 1948
Arab-Israeli War

An Undiplomatic Shuttle

**To the great people of the Government of Israel –
Egypt, excuse me.**
US President Gerald Ford, proposing a toast to Egyptian
President Anwar el-Sadat, 28 October 1975

**The Persian Gulf is the arsehole of the world, and
Basra is 80 miles up it.**
Harry Hopkins (1889–1946)

**I think the Kuwaitis enjoy a crisis now and again. It
brings them world attention.**
Barzan al-Takriti, Iraqi diplomat, in 1994, regarding rumours of
a second Iraqi invasion of Kuwait

**I am inconsolable at the death of King Hussein of
Jordan. I was a very good friend of Jordan: he was the
greatest basketball player this country has ever seen
or will see again.**
Mariah Carey, US pop singer, confusing the recently defunct
monarch of the Hashemite Kingdom with the American
basketball star Michael Jordan

One man's Mede is another man's Persian.
George S. Kaufman

No Alcohol in Iran

**An Iranian moderate is one who has run out of
ammunition.**
Henry Kissinger, in 1987

**The ayatollah is circumcised: there's no end
to the prick.**
Quoted in Nigel Rees, *Graffiti 2*

**No alcohol in Iran, but you can get stoned any time –
*And the Ayatollah Khomeini will shake you warmly by
the stump.***
Graffito

Egypt: The Paradise of Thieves

That's how the prison reformer Elizabeth Fry (1780–1845)
described the country.

**I never saw a place I liked worse, nor which afforded
less pleasure or instruction, nor antiquities which less
answered their description.**
James Bruce (1730–94)

Two Testicles or Three?

**In the days of the pharaohs, while working on the
hieroglyphic inscriptions on the tomb of the great
warrior Ramses II, one inscriber says to the other:
'Tell me, do you spell macho with two testicles or
three?'**
Internet joke

Cairo:

There is not perhaps upon the Earth a more dirty metropolis.

E.D. Clarke (1840–93)

The Pyramids:

A practical joke played on history.

Peter Forster (1818–86)

Israel: Four Million Prime Ministers

I will tell you that this nation of four million citizens is really an uneasy coalition of four million prime ministers.

Amos Oz, 'Israel', in *Granta* 17

If we lose this war, I'll start another in my wife's name.

Moshe Dayan, during the Six Day War, 1967

An American, a Russian and an Israeli are waiting to order in a restaurant. The waiter says, 'Excuse me, but I've got bad news. There's a shortage of meat.' The Russian asks, 'What's meat?' The American asks, 'What's a shortage?' The Israeli asks, 'What's excuse me?'

Internet joke

The Turk in All His Fatness Should Have Smoked

O Oliver, hadst thou been faithful ... the King of France should have bowed his neck under thee, the Pope should have withered as in winter, the Turk in all his fatness should have smoked.

George Fox, founder of the Quakers, to Oliver Cromwell, 1650s

Turkey was for long Christian Europe's top enemy, having placed most of southeastern Europe under the 'Ottoman yoke'.

Go to Constantinople and take the Turk by the beard.
William Shakespeare, *Henry V*, V.ii

Where the Turk's horse once treads, the grass never grows again.
English saying – echoed in the sayings of other countries: 'Where the Turk doth set foot, for a hundred years the soil brings forth no fruit' (German); 'No grass grows in the trail of the Turk' (Arab).

That were too cruel even for a Turk.
Dutch saying

Horatio Nelson on the Turks:
Perfectly useless.

In England the vices in fashion are whoring & drinking, in Turkey, sodomy and smoking.
Lord Byron, letter, 3 May 1810

**One of that saintly murderous brood
To carnage and the Koran given.**
Thomas Moore, *Lalla Rookh* (1817)

It's over, and can't be helped, and that's one consolation, as they always say in Turkey, ven they cut the wrong man's head off.
Sam Weller, in Charles Dickens's *Pickwick Papers* (1837)

The Sick Man of Europe

We have on our hands a sick man – a very sick man.
Tsar Nicholas I, referring to Turkey in a remark to Sir G.H.
Seymour, British envoy to St Petersburg, quoted in
Memoirs of Baron Stockmar (1853)

Before World War I, Turkey was known as the sick man of Europe. Now it is almost terminal.
Richard Nixon

Let the Turks now carry away their abuses in the only possible manner, namely by carrying off themselves. Their Zaptiehs and their Mudirs, their Bimbashis and their Yuzbachis, their Kaimakans and their Pashas, one and all, bag and baggage, shall, I hope, clear out from the province they have desolated and profaned.
W.E. Gladstone, pamphlet 'The Bulgarian Horrors and the Question of the East' (6 September 1876)

The unspeakable Turk.
Thomas Carlyle, letter to a meeting at St James's Hall, 1876

The Turk is an enemy who has never shown himself as good a fighter as the white man.
Anonymous British staff officer, before the Gallipoli landings, 1915. The Allied forces eventually had to withdraw in the face of stiff Turkish resistance.

Asia:
East is East

Oh, East is East, and West is West, and never the twain shall meet ...
Rudyard Kipling, 'The Ballad of East and West' (1892)

Holla, ye pampered jades of Asia!
Christopher Marlowe, *Tamburlaine the Great* (1590), part 2, IV.iii

The delirium and horror of the East. The dusty catastrophe of Asia. Green only on the banner of the Prophet. Nothing grows here except mustaches.
Joseph Brodsky, *Less Than One: Selected Essays,* 'Flight from Byzantium' (1986)

Asia is rich in people, rich in culture and rich in resources. It is also rich in trouble.
Hubert H. Humphrey, US vice-president, speech, 23 April 1966

The Civilized West?

Gandhi, when asked what he thought of Western civilization, replied:
It would be a good idea.

The View from the Raj

India is a geographical term. It is no more a united nation than the Equator.

Winston Churchill, speech, 18 March 1931

I suppose the real difficulty is an utter lack of courage, moral and political, amongst the natives.

King George V, letter to Lord Irwin, 10 March 1928

It is ... alarming and also nauseating to see Mr Gandhi, a seditious Middle Temple lawyer, now posing as a fakir of a type well known in the East, striding half-naked up the steps of the Viceregal Palace, while he is still organizing and conducting a defiant campaign of civil disobedience, to parley on equal terms with the representative of the King-Emperor.

Winston Churchill, speech to the West Essex Unionist Association, Epping, 23 February 1931. Gandhi had recently been released from prison to engage in talks about self-government.

A Short Tour of the Subcontinent

'Sub-' is no idle prefix in its application to this continent.

P.J. O'Rourke, 'Foreigners Around the World', in *National Lampoon*, 1976

First stop, Calcutta ...
The definition of obscenity.

Geoffrey Moorhouse

Loin Cloths and Other Mysteries of India

Chief amongst the mysteries of India is how the natives keep those little loin cloths up.

Robert Benchley (1889–1945), US humorist

There exists no politician in India daring enough to attempt to explain to the masses that cows can be eaten.

Indira Gandhi (1917–84), Indian prime minister

On to Delhi ...

Delhi is the capital of the losing streak. It is the metropolis of the crossed wire, the missed appointment, the puncture, the wrong number.

Jan Morris

Next stop, the Taj Mahal ...

How *was* the Taj Mahal? ... And it didn't look like a biscuit box did it? I've always felt that it might.

Amanda, in Noël Coward's *Private Lives* (1930)

Finally, to Pakistan ...

The sort of place everyone should send his mother-in-law for a month, all expenses paid.

Ian Botham, English cricketer, in a BBC Radio interview, March 1984. He was subsequently fined £1,000 by the Test and County Cricket Board for the remark.

Be Careful about Burma
(and Various Other Places)

Be careful about Burma. Most people cannot remember whether it was Siam and has become Thailand, or whether it is now part of Malaysia and should be called Sri Lanka.
Alexander Cockburn, 'How to be a Foreign Correspondent', in *More*, May 1976

Many decades earlier, the mad satanist Aleister Crowley had been unimpressed by the splendours of Burma:
Religion itself becomes offensively monotonous. On every point of vantage are pagodas – stupid stalagmites of stagnant piety.
The Confessions of Aleister Crowley (1929)

He was marginally better informed than Winston Churchill:
I have lived for 78 years without hearing of bloody places like Cambodia.

Outer Mongolia is such a *terra incognita* that Tibet is practically Coney Island by comparison.
James Gunther

And so to the South Koreans …
… too busy eating dogs to design a decent car.
Jeremy Clarkson, BBC motoring correspondent, in October 1998

And the North Koreans …
These cookies are beaten!
Major General Hobart Gay, in October 1950. It took another three years of fighting for US leaders to realize that the cookies weren't going to be beaten.

America's Vietnam

It's silly talking about how many years we will have to spend in the jungles of Vietnam when we could pave the whole country and put parking stripes on it and still be home for Christmas.
Ronald Reagan, interviewed in the *Fresno Bee*, 10 October 1965. Christmas 1973, as it turned out.

The previous year, President Lyndon Johnson had, with equal hubris, declared:
I didn't just screw Ho Chi Minh. I cut his pecker off.

In the end, though ...
To save the town it became necessary to destroy it.
US army major, referring to the bombing of Bentre in February 1968.

China: A Big Country, Inhabited by Many Chinese

China is a big country, inhabited by many Chinese.
Charles de Gaulle

Almost one out of every four people in the world is Chinese, you know, even though many of them might not look it.
Joseph Heller, *Good as Gold* (1979)

You'll end up with slitty eyes if you stay too long.
Prince Philip, to British students in China, 1986.
A Palace spokesman later explained that HRH
was concerned that strong sunlight might be
affecting them.

There are only two kinds of Chinese: those who give bribes and those who take them.
Russian saying

From time immemorial, China has had people who obey, and people who are thugs, but China has never had citizens.
Yu Jie, in the 1990s

Eating with Knitting Needles

You do not sew with a fork, and I see no reason why you should eat with knitting needles.
Miss Piggy, *Miss Piggy's Guide to Life (As Told to Henry Beard)* (1981)

The southern Chinese ... will eat almost anything ... Southerners themselves tell the story about the Indian and the Cantonese confronted by a creature from outer space: the Indian falls to his knees and begins to worship it, while the Chinese searches his memory for a suitable recipe.
Paul Levy, *Out to Lunch* (1986)

One might reverse *cave canem* – beware the dog – to 'dogs, beware'. No creature is safe, it seems:

Chinese civilization is so systematic that wild animals have been abolished on principle.
Aleister Crowley, *The Confessions of Aleister Crowley* (1929)

Birds in their little nests agree
With Chinamen, but not with me.
Hilaire Belloc, *On Food*, referring to bird's nest soup

Sheep and sow source.
The *Mirror*, headline, 28 March 2001, referring to the possible source of the British foot-and-mouth epidemic in pigswill from a Chinese restaurant

Japan: A Pure Invention

In fact, the whole of Japan is a pure invention. There is no such country, there are no such people ... The Japanese people are ... simply a mode of style, an exquisite fancy of art.
Oscar Wilde, 'The Decay of Lying' (1891)

The Japanese have perfected good manners and made them indistinguishable from rudeness.
Paul Theroux, *The Great Railway Bazaar* (1975)

The Japanese have almost as big a reputation for cruelty as do young children.
Dennis Bloodworth (1718–80)

Ants ... little yellow men who sit up all night thinking how to screw us.

Edith Cresson, French prime minister, on the Japanese in 1991

I had a good close-up, across the barbed wire, of various sub-human specimens dressed in dirty grey uniforms, which I was informed were Japanese soldiers ... I cannot believe they would form an intelligent fighting force.

Robert Brooke-Popham, air chief marshal and commander of British forces in the Far East, in December 1941. He was advising against strengthening Singapore's air defences. The city surrendered to the Japanese on 15 February 1942.

I don't greatly admire Japanese women; they have no figures to speak of, and look as if a bee had stung them in the eye.

Crosbie Garstin

Japanese food is very pretty and undoubtedly a suitable cuisine in Japan, which is largely populated by people of below average size. Hostesses hell-bent on serving such food to occidentals would be well advised to supplement it with something more substantial and to keep in mind that almost everybody likes French fries.

Fran Lebowitz, *Metropolitan Life* (1978)

The Japanese idea of fun is to lock a naked man in a room for eighteen months and allow him to exist only on food that he wins in competitions.

Emma Colverd

They have 21st-century bogs and 13th-century bog roll.
A.A. Gill, 'Mad in Japan', in the *Sunday Times* Magazine

When it comes to Japanese civilization, it's mostly eyewash. Kabuki theatre is only just preferable to root-canal work. The three-stringed guitar is a sad waste of cat ... The samurai were thugs in frocks with stupid haircuts, and haiku poems are limericks that don't make you laugh.
A.A. Gill, 'Mad in Japan', in the *Sunday Times* Magazine

Sex is where the weirdness of the Japanese peaks. I should start by saying that the widely held belief that you can buy soiled schoolgirls' knickers from vending machines is apocryphal, but it certainly could be true. It would hardly be out of character.
A.A. Gill, 'Mad in Japan', in the *Sunday Times* Magazine

If Freud had lived in Tokyo, we'd never have got analysis. He wouldn't have known where to start.
A.A. Gill, 'Mad in Japan', in the *Sunday Times* Magazine

Australia and Other Awful Antipodes

Outrageous Aussies and Dinkum Diggers

Australians have variously been known as *Aussies*, *Diggers* (from the gold rushes of the 19th century), *Dinkums*, *Gum-suckers* and *Kangaroos*.

Racial characteristics: violently loud alcoholic roughnecks whose idea of fun is to throw up on your car. The national sport is breaking furniture and the average daily consumption of beer in Sydney is ten and three-quarters imperial gallons for children under the age of nine.

P.J. O'Rourke, 'Foreigners Around the World', in *National Lampoon*, 1976

Where else in the world is a generous man defined as one who would give you his arsehole and shit through his ribs?

Germaine Greer, Australian feminist, in the *Sunday Times*, 1972

Australians are living proof that Aborigines screw kangaroos

Quoted in Nigel Rees, *The Guinness Dictionary of Jokes* (1995)

Bandicoot and Benaud

Australia! Land of strange, exotic creatures, freaks of evolution, ghastly victims of Mother Nature's vicious whimsy – kangaroo and platypus, potoroo and bandicoot, Richie Benaud ...

Peter Tinniswood, *The Brigadier Down Under* (1983)

It must be so pretty with all the dear little kangaroos flying about. Agatha has found it on the map. What a curious shape it is! Just like a large packing case.

The Duchess of Berwick, in Oscar Wilde's *Lady Windermere's Fan* (1892)

When I look at a map and see what an ugly country Australia is, I feel that I want to go there and see if it cannot be changed into a more beautiful form!

Oscar Wilde

In a way Australia is like Catholicism. The company is sometimes questionable and the landscape is grotesque. But you always come back.

Thomas Keneally, Australian novelist, in *Woman's Day*, 1983

I like Australia less and less. The hateful newness, the democratic conceit, every man a little pope of perfection.

D.H. Lawrence, letter, 28 May 1922

All Australians are an uneducated and unruly mob.
Douglas Jardine, English cricketer, commenting on the behaviour
of Australian spectators during the infamous 'Bodyline Tour' of
1932–3. In 1934 Sir Pelham Warner, the Trinidadian-born English
cricketer, wrote about Jardine to the governor of South Australia:
'He is a queer fellow. When he sees a cricket ground with an
Australian on it, he goes mad.'

Other Brits also lose all sense of proportion when confronted with
robust Australians. Paul Keating, Labour prime minister from 1991 to
1996, earned the following epithet from the *Sun* newspaper:
The Lizard of Oz.
Keating, an ardent republican, had given royalists the vapours
when he touched the Queen's arm during a royal visit.

One Big Penal Settlement

In 1788 the first European settlers arrived in Australia: 756 British
convicts.

**We're built, as a nation, on the grounds of a concentration
camp. It's like saying 'OK, here's Auschwitz. Here's where
we'll start our country.'**
Peter Carey, in *City Limits*, 1988

**I have been disappointed in all my expectations of
Australia, except as to its wickedness; for it is far more
wicked than I have conceived it possible for any place to
be, or than it is possible for me to describe to you in
England.**
Henry Parkes, English-born Australian statesman, letter,
1 May 1840

**Australia is still very exclusive ... On the visa
application they still ask if you've been convicted of a
felony – although they are willing to give you a visa
even if you haven't been.**
P.J. O'Rourke, *Holidays in Hell* (1988)

The English have never quite forgotten Australia's first
purpose:

That dreadful vulgar place.
The Duchess of Berwick, in Oscar Wilde's *Lady Windermere's
Fan* (1892)

**We had intended you to be
The next Prime Minister but three:
The stocks were sold; the Press was squared;
The Middle Class was quite prepared.
But as it is! ... My language fails!
Go out and govern New South Wales!**
Hilaire Belloc, *Cautionary Tales*, 'Lord Lundy' (1907)

The suspicion of 'bad blood' continued into the First
World War:
Get up, you lumps, and behave like Englishmen.
British officer to Aussie troops at Gallipoli

Gluttons for Culture

Q: **What's the difference between yoghurt and
Australia?**
A: **Yoghurt has a real live culture.**
Internet joke

***Xenophobia*: A love of Australia.**

Barry Humphries, glossary from *Bazza Pulls It Off* (1972)

***Australian-based*: A person of diminished aspiration who has been successfully bribed with grants and awards to resist the lure of expatriation.**

Barry Humphries, glossary from *A Nice Night's Entertainment* (1981)

***Koala Triangle*: A mysterious zone in the Southern Hemisphere where persons of talent disappear without trace.**

Barry Humphries, glossary from *A Nice Night's Entertainment*

So you're going to Australia? What are you going to sing? All I can say is sing 'em muck – it's all they understand.

Dame Nellie Melba, Australian opera singer, advising fellow singer Clara Butt

To live in Australia permanently is rather like going to a party and dancing all night with your mother.

Barry Humphries

The Australian mind, I can state with authority, is easily boggled.

Charles Osborne, in the *Daily Telegraph*, 1988

Australia is a huge rest home, where no unwelcome news is ever wafted on to the pages of the worst newspapers in the world.

Germain Greer, in the *Observer*, 1982

**Australia may be the only country in the world
in which the word 'academic' is regularly used
as a term of abuse.**

Dame Leonie Kramer

In Australia
Inter alia,
Mediocrities
Think they're Socrates.

Peter Porter, who claimed he had been denied a grant from the
Australian government as a result of writing these lines

**The only people really keeping the spirit of irony alive
in Australia are taxi-drivers and homosexuals.**

Barry Humphries, in *Australian Women's Weekly*,
February 1983

The Great Australian Adjective '——'

He plunged into the —— creek,
The —— horse was —— weak,
The stockman's face was a —— study!
And though the —— horse was drowned
The —— rider reached the ground
Ejaculating: ——!
——!

W.T. Goodge, *The Bulletin Reciter* (1940)

Tinnies and Tucker

One of the few moments of happiness a man knows in Australia is that moment of meeting the eyes of another man over the tops of two beer glasses.
Note found by Bruce Chatwin written on the flyleaf of a copy of *Tristram Shandy* in a second-hand bookstore in Alice Springs

How few Australians know anything about wines, and how very few drink anything regularly but vile, filthy whisky and gaseous, unwholesome beer.
George Meudell, *The Pleasant Career of a Spendthrift* (1929)

Fair Australia. Oh what a dump.
All you get to eat is crocodile,
Bandicoot's brains and catfish pie.
Let me go home again before I die.
Traditional, quoted in *The Ugly Australian* (1976)

Here is a description of the typical fare to be had in Australian eating houses:
Steak cut from drovers' old boots, limp shredded lettuce, one tomato slice ... Banana special, fruit salad and ice-cream, peach Melba.
Bill Olson, *National Times* (1975)

Games Devised for Padded Cells

Australian rules football might best be described as a game devised for padded cells, played in the open air.
Jim Murray, US sports writer

Without giving offence to anyone, I may remark that it [Australian rules football] is a game which commends itself to semi-barbarous races.
Edward Kinglake, 'The Australians at Home' (1891)

When you come back from touring Australia, you almost feel like you've been to Vietnam.
Glenn Turner, New Zealand-born cricketer, in 1983, recovering from the 'sledging' dealt out by the Aussie players

Anyone who does not watch rugby league is not a real person. He's a cow's hoof, an ethnic or comes from Melbourne.
John Singleton, *Australian* (1981)

New Zealand: Kiwis and Pig Islanders

The term *Pig Island* for New Zealand dates from the time that Captain Cook introduced pigs there.

Asked what he thought of New Zealand, Clement Freud said:
I find it hard to say, because when I was there, it seemed to be shut.
Attributed to various others over the years

Terrible Tragedy in the South Seas. Three million people trapped alive!
Tom Scott, in the *Listener*, 1979

New Zealand Europeans, and I am not saying this in a bitter way, are peasants. What we have here is aristocratic Maoris and peasant Europeans.
Peter Tapsall, Maori minister of internal affairs, in 1985

EPILOGUE

The Last Refuge of the Scoundrel

Patriotism is the last refuge of a scoundrel.
Samuel Johnson, on 7 April 1775, quoted in James Boswell, *The Life of Samuel Johnson* (1791)

Just to prove Johnson's point:
My rackets are run on strictly American lines and they're going to stay that way!
Al Capone

Love makes fools, marriage cuckolds, and patriotism malevolent imbeciles.
Paul Léautaud, French critic, *Passe-temps* (1929)

Patriotism is often an arbitrary veneration of real estate above principles.
George Jean Nathan

Patriotism is the virtue of the vicious.
Oscar Wilde

'My country, right or wrong' is a thing no patriot would ever think of saying except in a desperate case. It is like saying, 'My mother, drunk or sober.'
G.K. Chesterton, *The Defendant* (1901)

Patriotism is as fierce as a fever, pitiless as the grave, blind as a stone, and irrational as a headless hen.

Ambrose Bierce (1842–?1914)

Nationalism: The Measles of Mankind

Nationalism is an infantile disease. It is the measles of mankind.

Albert Einstein, letter, 1921

This barbarous feeling of nationality ... has become the curse of Europe.

W. Nassau Senior, British economist, diary, 20 May 1850

The nationalist has a broad hatred and a narrow love. He cannot stifle a predilection for dead cities.

André Gide, *Journals*, 1918

Nationalism is a silly cock crowing on its own dunghill.

Richard Aldington, *The Colonel's Daughter* (1931)

Nationalism is our form of incest, is our idolatry, is our insanity. 'Patriotism' is its cult.

Erich Fromm, *The Sane Society* (1955)

I am always fascinated when people talk about 'the forging of a nation'. Most nations are forgeries, perpetrated in the last century or so.

Neal Ascherson, in the *Observer*, 1985

A Common Hatred of Our Neighbours

A nation is a society united by a delusion about its ancestry and by a common hatred of its neighbours.

Dean William R. Inge

Altogether, national hatred is something peculiar. You will always find it strongest and most violent where there is the lowest degree of culture.

Goethe, quoted in J.P. Eckermann, *Conversations with Goethe*, 14 March 1830

Admiration for ourselves and our institutions is too often measured by our contempt and dislike for foreigners.

William Ralph Ince, *Outspoken Essays: First Series*, 'Patriotism' (1919)

I am free of all prejudice. I hate everyone equally.

W.C. Fields (1879–1946)

PICTURE CREDITS

166–7 British politician, James Thomas (1874–1949), enjoying a long smoke with friends, *c.*1935 (Hulton/Getty Images).

175 Skinhead (Hulton/Getty Images).

192–3 Michael O'Brien streaking at a rugby match between England and France at Twickenham in 1974 (Syndication International/Ian Bradshaw).

200 Tom Jones during a guest performance in Shirley MacLean's show on 24 April 1979 (Hulton/Getty Images).

208–9 Scotland v England (Rex Features/Today).

222–3 Smoking nuns (Hulton/Getty Images).

242 Baseball fan drinking from a beer hat during a game between the Cleveland Indians and the Seattle Mariners on 18 June 1986 (Corbis/Bettmann).

254–5 Miss Nude California in 1979 (Rex Features/Jim Selby).

262–3 The McGuire brothers sitting astride two motorbikes during their tour of Japan in the 1970s. Their mission in Japan was to take on anybody they thought was big enough to try and throw either of the two men (Hulton/Getty Images).

274–5 George W. Bush reacting to a turkey named Liberty at the annual turkey pardoning event at the White House, three days ahead of Thanksgiving on 19 November 2001. The fortunate bird will spend the rest of his days on a farm in Virginia (Popperfoto/Reuters/Kevin LaMargue).

290 Argentinian Wall, 2 June 2002 (Popperfoto/Reuters).

302–3 Iranian veiled women training on the outskirts of Tehran, February 1986. (Magnum Photos/Jean Gaumy).

310 A pig being transported on a bicycle to market in Guangzhou in China (Rex Features).

323 Barry Humphries at Madame Tussaud's at the unveiling of the wax figure of Dame Edna Everage. Humphries conducted the proccedings in his role of Sir Leslie Patterson (Popperfoto/UPI).